Fodor's Budapest

FIRST EDITION

Fodor's Travel Publications, Inc.
New York • London • Toronto

Fodor's Budapest

Editor: Christopher Billy
Contributors: Richard W. Bruner, Robert Blake, Alan Levy, Linda K. Schmidt, Julie Tomasz
Art Director: Fabrizio La Rocca
Cartographer: David Lindroth
Illustrator: Karl Tanner
Cover Photograph: Richard Marshall

Design: Vignelli Associates

Special Sales

Contents

Maps

Foreword

We wish to express our gratitude to Erika Pollák of the Hungarian Tourist Board in Budapest for her constant interest and advice as well as her unremitting quest for accuracy. Special thanks are also due to Richard and Erzsébet Bruner for their help with fact checking and last-minute updates.

While every care has been taken to ensure the accuracy of the information in this guide, the passage of time will always bring change, and consequently, the publisher cannot accept responsibility for errors that may occur.

All prices and opening times quoted here are based on information supplied to us at press time. Hours and admission fees may change, however, and the prudent traveler will avoid inconvenience by calling ahead.

Fodor's wants to hear about your travel experiences, both pleasant and unpleasant. When a hotel or restaurant fails to live up to its billing, let us know and we will investigate the complaint and revise our entries where the facts warrant it.

Send your letters to the editors of Fodor's Travel Publications, 201 E. 50th Street, New York, NY 10022.

Highlights
and
Fodor's Choice

Highlights

The most important thing that has happened to Hungary since it became a multiparty parliamentary democracy in 1990 is, without doubt, its winning of associate status in the **European Community** (EC) in 1991. Possibly not since King Mátyás Hunyadi and his wife, Beatrice of Aragon, sought to bring the Renaissance to this central European country has an independent Hungary taken such a significant step into a fraternity of nations. The impact of the event on the future economy of Hungary cannot be overstated. Because Hungary's economy must be export-driven, EC status will help pull the country out of the socialist doldrums into a community of industrial democracies.

Income from tourism is another crucial factor in Hungary's improved situation. In the past, Hungary depended on Soviet-bloc citizens for tourism. Now the country gets more tourists from the West and welcomes them with open arms because they, of course, are more affluent. Last year, Germany, France, and Austria led the Western countries in the number of tourists coming to Hungary.

Another important development whose impact is hard to overstate is the **privatization** of the nation's state-owned businesses. Last year the State Property Agency (SPA) sold off more than half a billion dollars worth of state-owned enterprises, at least 30% to Western investors.

Hungary has earned a reputation for good management. *Euromoney,* a London-based financial magazine, chose the National Bank of Hungary as the "loan raiser" of 1991. The bank's president said the distinction implied that the international capital market was confident that Hungary would be able to repay its debts; this designation reinforced the president's conviction that there is simply no alternative to good debt management. Hungary is unusual among former East-bloc countries in that it has never asked its creditors to reschedule or eliminate any of its $20 billion debt.

Thus Hungary is gradually becoming Westernized, partly through the growth of Western-owned companies with interests in the country (such as General Electric, General Motors, and Ford) and partly through the expatriate community. After delays caused by the confused state of property ownership, major construction is finally under way. Two examples are the German-owned **Kempinski Hotel** being built near Deák tér in downtown Buda and the new office building to be built near the American embassy on Szabadság tér, whose owners will include Olympia and York, an American firm.

Budapest has long been proud of the fact that more of the major luxury and business-class hotel chains are represented here than in any of the Central European capitals, Vienna included. Many of these hotels—the **Hyatt, Hilton, Ramada,** and **InterContinental,** for example—were already in operation before the collapse of Hungary's communist government. Despite the fact that many of these establishments first opened their doors in the '80s, almost all are renovating at least some of their facilities in order to compete more effectively for the growing number of increasingly discriminating tourists. Even the 12-year-old **Forum,** which in 1985 was named American Express Hotel of the Year in Europe and the Middle East, recently remodeled its guest rooms. Among recent additions to Budapest's hotel scene are the **Flamenco** (1989), a quiet luxury hotel off the beaten track next to a park in the Buda foothills; the **Helia** (1990), postcommunist Hungary's first privately built major hotel; and the **Aquincum** (1991), an elaborate spa hotel just north of downtown Buda.

One problem that will plague Hungary (and the rest of post-socialist Europe) for a long time is **pollution.** Automobiles without catalytic converters, electric-generating plants that still burn soft coal, and other factories without adequate waste disposal and scrubbers are the source of grave environmental problems. Today, alongside the countless taxis, Ladas, and infamous East German Trabants careening through the streets of Pest, more and more Hungarian-owned Western cars contribute to the terrible traffic congestion and related pollution problems. The good news is that Hungary's parliament is now considering passing an environmental-protection law, drafted by a Hungarian law professor who spent time at a New York law school and modeled his bill after the best antipollution legislation in effect in the Western world. Budapest also has the advantage of being the headquarters for the U.S.-financed Regional Environmental Center for Central & Eastern Europe, which is helping environmental movements in the entire region to push for better legislation.

Fodor's Choice

No two people will agree on what makes a perfect vacation, but it's fun and helpful to know what others think. We hope you'll have a chance to experience some of Fodor's Choices yourself while visiting Budapest. For detailed information about each entry, refer to the appropriate chapters within this guidebook.

Hotels

Atrium Hyatt *(Very Expensive)*

Duna InterContinental (Very Expensive)

Forum *(Very Expensive)*

Béke Radisson *(Expensive)*

Gellért *(Expensive)*

Helia *(Expensive)*

Thermal *(Expensive)*

Astoria *(Moderate)*

Erzsébet *(Moderate)*

Taverna *(Moderate)*

Restaurants

Alabárdos *(Very Expensive)*

Gundel *(Very Expensive)*

Légrádi Testvérek *(Very Expensive)*

Paradiso *(Very Expensive)*

Baroque *(Expensive)*

Fortuna *(Expensive)*

Postakocsi *(Expensive)*

Duna-Corso *(Moderate)*

Kaltenberg *(Moderate)*

Kis Buda *(Moderate)*

Kehli *(Inexpensive)*

Nightlife

Fortuna

Fregatt

Horoszkop

Pierrot

Museums and Galleries

Castle District Museums (Várhegy)

Mũcsarnok (Art Gallery)

Szépmũvészeti Múzeum (Museum of Fine Arts)

Walks

Margaret Island

The riverbank near the parliament building in Pest

The castle district in Buda (Várhegy)

The length of Andrássy út from downtown to Heroes' Square

The City Park beyond Heroes' Square

Váci utca

Buildings and Special Sights

The Roman ruins and Archaeological Museum at Aquincum (Chapters 2 and 3)

Parliament (Országház)

Heroes' Square (Hõsök tere)

Royal Palaca (Királyi Palota)

Fishermen's Bastion (Halászbástya)

Gellért Hill

Hungarian Television Headquarters

Keleti Pályaudvar (East Railway station)

Chain Bridge (Széchenyi lánchíd)

Churches and Temples

Great Synagogue

St. Stephen's Basilica (Szent István Bazilika)

Matthias Church of Budavar (Mátyás templom)

Taban Parish Church (Tabán plébánia-templom)

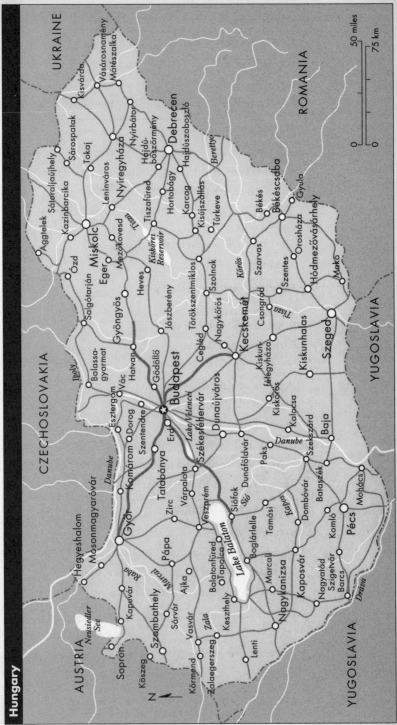

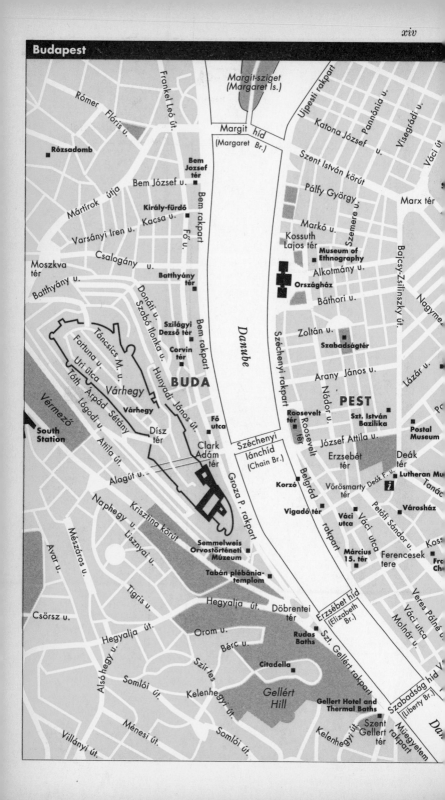

Lehel
tér

Szépművészeti
Múzeum

Hősök tere

Hősök
tere

Mücsarnok

Városliget

Rippl-Rónai u.

Dózsa György út

Olof Palme sétány

Élmunkás híd

Szinyei Merse u.

Bajza u.

Benczúr u.

Ajtósi Dürer sor

West
Station

Rudas László utca

Szondi u.

Rózsa Ferenc u.

Felső erdősor

Gorkij fasor

Dózsa György út

Teréz körút (Lenin körút)

Aradi u.

Jókai u.

Liszt Memorial
Museum

Damjanich u.

Dembinszky u.

...ó u.

Andrássy (Népköztársaságl) út

Vörösmarty u.

Rottenbiller utca

Landler Jenő u.

Opera
House

Liszt Academy
of Music

Erzsébet körút

Hársfa u.

Thököly út.

Verseny u.

East
Station

...aulay Ede u.

Király (Majakovszkij) u.

Klauzál u.

Baross
tér

Kerepesi út.

Dob utca

Wesselény utca

Rákóczi út.

Mező Imre út.

Kerepesi
Temető
Cemetery

...useum

Dohány utca

Köztársaság
tér

N

...cs krt.

Great
Synagogue

Rákóczi út.

József körút

Népszínház u.

Teleki
László
tér

Luiza u.

...suth L. u.

Szenkirályi u.

St. Roch
Chapel

Somogyi Béla u.

Bérkocsis u.

Déri Miksa u.

Mátyás
tér

Dankó u.

...ranciscan
...hurch

Puskin u.

Bródy Sándor u.

József u.

Egyetem
tér

Múzeum krt.

National
Museum

Múzeum u.

Krúdy u.

Baross utca

Kálvin
tér

Baross utca

Diószeghy Sámuel

...s u.

Üllői út.

Nap u.

Szigony u.

Vámház krt.

Lónyai u.

Ráday u.

Práter u.

Fővám tér.

Iparmuveszeti
Museum

Tömő u.

Korányi S. u.

Danube

Közraktár u.

Ferenc körút

| 0 | 550 yards |
| 0 | 500 meters |

World Time Zones

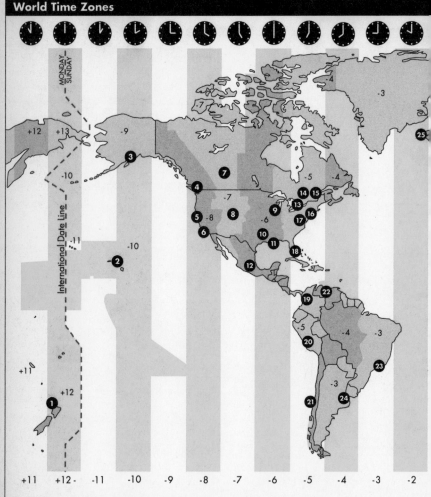

Numbers below vertical bands relate each zone to Greenwich Mean Time (0 hrs.).
Local times frequently differ from these general indications,
as indicated by light-face numbers on map.

Introduction

Divided by the Danube into hilly, romantic Buda and the businesslike plain of Pest, Budapest has suffered many ravages in its long history. It was totally destroyed by the Mongols in 1241, captured by the Turks in 1541, and nearly destroyed again by Soviet troops in World War II. But this bustling industrial and cultural center survived as the capital of the People's Republic of Hungary after the war—and then, as the '80s drew to a close, it became one of the Eastern bloc's capitals of capitalism.

Long the least rigid of the Eastern-bloc nations—Hungary had no daily currency-exchange minimums, and visas were always easy to come by—Hungary was the first to physically dismantle the Iron Curtain (ceremoniously cutting its barbed wire in 1989) and the first to break politically with communism.

In 1989 it also changed its foreign-investment law, opening the door to foreign ownership of as much as 100% of an enterprise. An American Chamber of Commerce was formed by 57 U.S. companies doing business in Hungary. The official state travel agency, IBUSZ, went public on the Vienna Stock Exchange and sold shares through Austrian banks. For Budapest businesses both large and small, the magic word these days is "privatization." In the absence of legislation limiting disposal of state-owned assets, privatization has proceeded apace. Hungary's fervent embrace of capitalism makes Budapest perhaps the easiest and most comfortable Eastern-bloc city in which to do business.

Despite Western aid and investment, the consequences of Soviet-style *perestroika* (restructuring) seem to be, at least temporarily, devaluation and inflation. For foreign visitors, the best advice is to exchange currency every day or two and use credit cards, which can produce hefty discounts at billing time. For average Hungarians, however, soaring inflation coupled with modest salaries vastly curb their ability to purchase the new luxury goods that are becoming available. As a result, store owners generally stock their shelves with expensive goods geared toward the Western buyer, and the prices are marked up accordingly.

Although prices are expected to steadily climb here, Budapest remains a vacation bargain by Western standards. Away from the touristy shopping districts in the capital, the prices for food, museums, outdoor recreation, and lodging remain low.

1 Essential Information

Before You Go

Government Tourist Offices

Hungarian Travel Bureau (IBUSZ). In North America: 1 Parker Pl., Fort Lee, NJ 07024, tel. 201/592–8585.

In the United Kingdom: 6 Conduit St., London W1R 9TG, tel. 071/493–0263.

Tour Groups

If you're traveling to Eastern Europe for the first time, you might want to consider a group tour. Escorted motor-coach tours provide comprehensive sightseeing coverage of the area's modern cities, ancient villages, and historic sites. Most escorted tours team Budapest with a number of other Eastern European cities, such as Prague, Warsaw, Moscow, St. Petersburg, Sofia, and Bucharest, giving you an efficient overview of their most famous sights and attractions. Several operators, however, offer tours dedicated to the exploration of Hungary's ancient capital.

Keep in mind that when choosing a group tour you must march to the beat of the tour guide's drum. If freedom and flexibility are more important, or if you're returning to Eastern Europe for a second time, consider an independent package. Many tour operators offer special deals that let you custom-design your own itinerary, choosing hotels from an à la carte menu or assembling mini hotel packages. For a balance of flexibility and structure, you can follow a prearranged itinerary independently, participating in optional planned activities along the way.

When evaluating any tour, be sure to find out exactly what expenses are included (particularly tips, taxes and service charges, side trips, additional meals, and entertainment); ratings of all hotels on the itinerary and the facilities they offer; cancellation policies for both you and the tour operator; and, if you are traveling alone, the cost for a single supplement.

The following list of operators and packages will give you an idea of what is available. For additional resources, contact your travel agent or the tourist offices of the countries you plan to visit. Most tour operators request that bookings be made through a travel agent, and there is no additional charge for doing so.

General-interest Tours
U.S.-based

Caravan Tours (401 N. Michigan Ave., Chicago, IL 60611, tel. 312/321–9800) covers Budapest, Vienna, Prague, Moscow, and Leningrad in 15 days.

General Tours (770 Broadway, New York, NY 10003, tel. 212/598–1800 or 800/221–2216) combines Budapest and Prague on a nine-day tour, which features comprehensive city sightseeing plus excursions to Konopiště and Lidice in Czechoslovakia and the Danube Bend in Hungary.

Love Holidays/Uniworld (15315 Magnolia Blvd., Sherman Oaks, CA 91403, tel. 818/501–6868) teams up Budapest with Vienna on a weeklong tour.

Maupintour (Box 807, Lawrence, KA 66044, tel. 800/255–4266 or 913/843–1211) gives you a week to get acquainted with Budapest. Sightseeing includes full-day excursions through Eger and the Matra mountains, the Danube Bend, and the districts of Buda and Pest.

Olson-Travelworld (100 N. Sepulveda Blvd., Suite 1010, El Segundo, CA 90245, tel. 800/421–2255, 800/421–5785 in CA or 213/615–0711) teams Budapest with other Eastern European cities such as Warsaw, Krakow, and Prague on a 17-day tour.

Other operators that include Budapest on their Eastern European itineraries are **Delta Dream Vacations** (tel. 800/338–2010 or 305/522–1440), **Trafalgar Tours** (21 E. 26th St., New York, NY 10010, tel. 800/854–0103 or 212/689–8977), and **TWA Getaway Vacations** (tel. 800/GETAWAY).

U.K.-based **Danube Travel Ltd.** (6 Conduit St., London W1R 9TG, tel. 071/493–0263) offers packages to Budapest for three or more nights, with optional excursions from the city, and will make arrangements for the Budapest Spring Festival and Hungarian Grand Prix.

Hamilton Travel Ltd. (3 Heddon St., London W1R 7LE, tel. 071/437–4627) offers flight/accommodation packages for one or more nights to Budapest.

Intasun (Intasun House, 2 Cromwell Ave., Bromley, Kent BR2 9AQ, tel. 081/466–4567 or Bradford 0274/736–403) features Budapest in a three-, four-, or seven-night, twin-center holiday with Vienna.

Sovereign Cities (Groundstar House, London Rd., Crawley, West Sussex RH10 2TB, tel. 0293/561–444) offers flight/hotel packages from two to seven nights, with a guided tour of the city and optional excursions.

Thomson Holidays (Greater London House, Hampstead Rd., London NW1 7SD, tel. 071/387–6534) offers three-, four-, and seven-night packages to Budapest, with an optional city tour and Danube Bend excursion. A twin-center holiday including Vienna is also available.

Time Off Ltd. (Chester Close, Chester St., London SW1X 7BQ, tel. 071/235–8070) offers packages to Budapest from two to seven nights with optional sightseeing excursions.

Travelscene Ltd. (Travelscene House, 11–15 St. Ann's Road, Harrow, Middlesex HA1 1AS, tel. 081/427–4445) offers three-, five-, and seven-night flight/hotel packages to Budapest with optional excursions.

Package Deals for Independent Travelers

American Airlines Fly AAway Vacations (tel. 800/433–7300 or 817/355–1234) offers an eight-day Budapest package, including round-trip air transportation and a half-day sightseeing tour. A three-day package is also available.

American Express Vacations (Box 5014, Atlanta, GA 30302, tel. 800/241–1700; or in GA, 800/282–0800) offers a 10-day independent tour of Budapest, Prague, and Vienna.

Delta Dream Vacations (Box 1525, Fort Lauderdale, FL 33302, tel. 800/221–6666, ext. 4122) offers 10-day to 22-day tours of Eastern Europe. Budapest is included in almost all itineraries.

General Tours (770 Broadway, New York, NY 10003, tel. 212/598–1800 or 800/221–2216) offers a two-night package, including half-day sightseeing, dinner at a local restaurant, and round-trip airport transfers. Full-day excursions to the Danube Bend, Lake Balaton, and the *puszta* plains are also available via private car.

Globetrotters (139 Main St., Cambridge, MA 02142, tel. 800/999–0970 or 617/621–9911) has an 11-day independent tour of Budapest, Prague, and Vienna, including round-trip airfare and first-class train transportation between cities. The company also gives you preferred hotel rates; stay for just one night or as many as you choose.

Travel Bound (599 Broadway, New York, NY 10012, tel. 800/456–8656 or 212/334–1350) gives you three nights in Vienna and three in Budapest, including round-trip airfare, rail transportation between the two cities, and half-day city tours. Preferred rates at hotels in Budapest are also available when you book three nights.

When to Go

Many of Hungary's major fairs and festivals take place in the spring and fall. During July and August, Budapest can be hot and the resorts at Lake Balaton crowded, so spring (May) and the end of summer (September) are the ideal times to visit.

Climate The following are the average daily maximum and minimum temperatures for Budapest.

Jan.	34F	1C	May	72F	22C	Sept.	73F	23C
	25	−4		52	11		54	12
Feb.	39F	4C	June	79F	26C	Oct.	61F	16C
	28	−2		59	15		45	7
Mar.	50F	10C	July	82F	28C	Nov.	46F	8C
	36	2		61	16		37	3
Apr.	63F	17C	Aug.	81F	27C	Dec.	39F	4C
	45	7		61	16		30	−1

Current weather information for more than 750 cities around the world may be obtained by calling WeatherTrak information service at 900/370–8728 (cost: 95¢ per minute). A taped message will tell you to dial the three-digit access code for the area in which you're interested. The code is either the area code (in the United States) or the first three letters of the foreign city. For a list of all access codes, send a stamped, self-addressed envelope to Cities, 9B Terrace Way, Greensboro, NC 27403. For more information, call 800/247–3282.

What to Pack

Clothing Don't worry about packing lots of formal clothing. Fashion was all but nonexistent under communism, and Western dress of any kind is considered stylish. A sport jacket for men, and a dress or pants for women, is appropriate for an evening out in Budapest. Everywhere else, you'll feel comfortable in casual corduroys or jeans.

Most of Budapest and the surrounding countryside is best seen on foot, so take a pair of sturdy walking shoes and be prepared to use them. If you plan on touring the hilly terrain along the Danube Bend or the northern shore of Lake Balaton, be sure the shoes have good traction and ankle support, as some of the trails can be quite challenging.

Miscellaneous Many items that you take for granted at home are either occasionally unavailable or of questionable quality in Hungary. Take your own toiletries and personal hygiene products with you. Women should pack tampons or sanitary napkins, which are in short supply. If you plan on doing any sports, bear in mind that few places have equipment for rent. An alternative to bringing your own equipment would be to buy what you need locally and take it home with you. In general, sporting goods are relatively cheap and of good quality. You will need an electrical adapter for small appliances; the voltage is 220, with 50 cycles.

Carry-on Luggage Airlines generally allow each passenger one piece of carry-on luggage on international flights from the United States. The bag cannot exceed 45 inches (length + width + height) and must fit under the seat or in the overhead luggage compartment.

Checked Luggage Passengers are generally allowed to check two pieces of luggage, neither of which can exceed 62 inches (length + width + height) or weigh more than 70 pounds. Baggage allowances vary slightly among airlines, so check with the carrier or your travel agent before departure.

Taking Money Abroad

Traveler's checks are generally impractical for everyday use, because only the larger banks or exchange offices know what to do with them. So be sure to bring some cash along, too. Once you exchange your money into Hungarian forints, it may be difficult to exchange it back into Western currency when you leave. Therefore, bring smaller denominations and exchange only as needed. Credit cards are helpful, too, and are accepted by many of the better hotels and restaurants. But a surprising number of hotels, especially outside Budapest, still don't take them, so always carry enough cash with you to cover at least a night's stay.

Traveler's checks and major U.S. credit cards, particularly American Express, are accepted in larger cities and resorts. In smaller towns and rural areas you may need cash. You won't get as good an exchange rate at home as abroad, but it's wise to change a small amount of money before you go; lines at airport currency-exchange booths can be very long. If your local bank can't change your currency, you can exchange money through Thomas Cook Currency Services. To find the office nearest you, contact them at 29 Broadway, New York, NY 10006 (tel. 212/757–6915).

For safety and convenience, it's always best to take traveler's checks. The most widely recognized traveler's checks are American Express, Barclay's, Thomas Cook, and those issued through major commercial banks such as Citibank and Bank of America. Some banks will issue checks free to established customers, but most of them charge a 1% commission fee. Buy several traveler's checks in small denominations to cash toward the end of your trip. This will save you from having to cash a large check and ending up with more foreign money than you need. (Hold on to your receipts after exchanging your traveler's checks; it's easier to convert foreign currency back into dollars if you have the receipts.) Remember to take the addresses of offices where you can get refunds for lost or stolen traveler's checks. *The American Express Traveler's Companion* is a worldwide directory of offices to contact in case of loss or theft of American Express traveler's checks. It is available at most travel-service locations.

Getting Money from Home

There are at least three ways to get to money from home:

(1) Have it sent through a large commercial bank that has a branch in the town where you're staying. The only drawback is that you must have an account with the bank; otherwise, you'll have to go through your own bank, and the process will be slower and more expensive.

(2) Have it sent through American Express. If you are a cardholder, you can cash a personal check or a counter check at an American Express office for up to $1,000 ($2,500 for gold cardholders) in cash or traveler's checks (there is a 1% commission on traveler's checks). American Express also provides another service, and you don't have to be a cardholder to use it: the American Express MoneyGram. You will have to call home and have someone go to an American Express office or MoneyGram agent and fill out the necessary form. The amount sent must be in increments of $50 and must be paid for with cash, MasterCard or Visa, or the Optima card. The American Express MoneyGram agent authorizes the transfer of funds to an American Express office in the town where you're staying. You'll need to show identification when picking up the money, and you must know the transaction reference number. The money will be available in 5 to 10 minutes and can be picked up at the American Express office in Budapest. Fees vary according to the amount of money sent. For sending $500, the fee is $45; for $1,000 it is $70. For more information or to locate the nearest American Express MoneyGram agent nearest you call 800/543–4080.

(3) Have it sent through Western Union (tel. 800/325–6000). If you have a MasterCard or Visa, you can have money sent for any amount up to your credit limit. If not, have someone take cash or a certified cashier's check to a Western Union office. The money will be available at the National Bank of Hungary in Budapest in one to two days. Fees vary with the amount of money being sent. For $1,000 the fee is around $75, for $500 it is $65.

Hungarian Currency

The unit of currency is the forint (Ft.), divided into 100 fillérs (f.). There are bills of 20, 50, 100, 500, and 1,000 and coins of 10, 20, and 50 fillérs and of 1, 2, 5, 10, and 20 forints. The tourist exchange rate was approximately 60 to the dollar and 100 to the pound sterling at press time (fall 1991), but these rates are likely to change during 1992. Note that official exchange rates are adjusted every Tuesday.

Hungary does not require you to exchange a certain sum of money for each day of your stay. Exchange money as you need it at banks, hotels, or travel offices—but not too much. Although in theory you can change back 50% (up to U.S. $100) of the original sum when you leave, it may prove difficult in practice.

Most credit cards are accepted, but don't rely on them in smaller towns or at less expensive accommodations and restaurants. Eurocheque holders can cash personal checks in all banks and in most hotels.

There is a black market in currency, but you will not gain much and could lose a good deal by taking advantage of it. It is still illegal to give or sell hard currency to a Hungarian. Although you may bring in any amount of foreign currency, you may bring in no more than 100 Ft. in coins (no bills).

What It Will Cost

Although first-class hotel chains in Budapest charge standard international prices, quality hotels are still modest by Western standards. The introduction of value-added tax (VAT) in 1988 has increased many of the prices in the service industry by up to 25%, and the annual inflation rate of 30% keeps creeping higher. Nevertheless, enjoyable vacations with all the trimmings still remain relatively inexpensive.

Sample Costs A cup of coffee will cost about 20–45 Ft.; a bottle of beer, 50–75 Ft.; soft drinks, 20–50 Ft.; a ham sandwich, 100 Ft.; one-mile taxi ride, 50 Ft.; museum admission, 15–60 Ft.

Passports and Visas

Americans A visa is not required to enter Hungary. A valid passport is sufficient for stays of up to 90 days. For additional information, contact the Hungarian Embassy, 3910 Shoemaker St. NW, Washington, DC 20008, tel. 202/362–6730.

To obtain a passport, apply in person; renewals can be obtained in person or by mail. First-time applicants should apply to one of the 13 U.S. Passport Agency offices at least five weeks in advance of their departure date. In addition, local county courthouses, many state and probate courts, and some post offices accept passport applications. Necessary documents include: (1) a completed passport application (Form DSP-11); (2) proof of citizenship (birth certificate with raised seal or naturalization papers); (3) proof of identity (unexpired driver's license, employee ID card, military ID, student ID, or any other document with your photograph and signature); (4) two recent, identical, two-inch-square photographs (black and white or color); (5) a $42 application fee for a 10-year passport (those under 18 pay $27 for a five-year passport). Passports are mailed to you in about 10-15 working days. If you are paying in cash, you must have exact change; no change is given. To renew your passport by mail, you'll need to send a completed Form DSP-82, two recent, identical passport photographs, your current passport (less than 12 years old), and a check or money order for $35.

If your passport is lost or stolen abroad, report it immediately to the nearest U.S. embassy or consulate and to local police authorities. If you can provide the consular officer with the information contained in the passport, they will most likely be able to issue you a new passport. For this reason, it is a good idea to keep a copy of the data page of your passport in a separate place, or leave the passport number, date, and place of issuance with a relative or friend in the United States.

Canadians Canadian citizens must have a valid passport and a visa to enter Hungary. To obtain a visa, you must have a passport, two photographs, and a single-entry visa, which is valid for one month. A multiple-entry visa costs $60 and is valid for one year. Contact your nearest embassy for details.

To acquire a passport, send a completed application (available at any post office or passport office) to the Bureau of Passports, Suite 215, West Tower, Guy Favreau Complex, 200 Rene Levesque Boulevard West, Montreal, Quebec H2Z 1X4. Include $25, two photographs, a guarantor, and proof of Canadian citizenship. Applications can be made in person at regional passport offices in many locations, including Edmonton, Halifax, Montreal, Toronto, Vancouver, and Winnipeg. Passports are valid for five years and are not renewable.

Britons You need a valid 10-year passport to enter Hungary (cost: £15 for a standard 32-page passport, £30 for a 94-page passport). Application forms are available from most travel agents and major post offices and from the Passport Office (Clive House, 70 Petty France, London SW1H 9HD, tel. 071/279–3434 for recorded information, or 071/279–4000). A British Visitors Passport is not acceptable. A visa is no longer required.

Customs and Duties

On Departure If you are bringing any foreign-made equipment from home, such as cameras, it's wise to carry the original receipt or register it with U.S. Customs before you leave (Form 4457). Otherwise you may end up paying duty on your return.

On Arrival If you are over 16 you may bring in 250 cigarettes or 50 cigars or 250 grams of tobacco; two liters of wine and one liter of spirits; 60 milliliters of perfume; and small gifts not exceeding a value of 1,000 Ft. each, to a total value of 10,000 Ft.

U.S. Customs You may bring home duty-free up to $400 worth of foreign goods, as long as you have been out of the country for at least 48 hours and you haven't claimed that exemption in the past 30 days. Each member of your family is entitled to the same exemption, regardless of age, and exemptions may be pooled. For the next $1,000 worth of goods, a flat 10% rate is assessed; above $1,400, duties vary with the merchandise. Included in the allowances for travelers 21 or older are one liter of alcohol, 100 cigars (non-Cuban), and 200 cigarettes. Only one bottle of perfume trademarked in the United States may be imported. There is no duty on antiques or works of art over 100 years old. Anything exceeding these limits will be taxed at the port of entry and may be taxed additionally in the traveler's home state. Gifts valued at under $50 may be mailed duty-free to friends or relatives at home, but you may not send more than one package per day to a single addressee, and packages may not include perfumes costing more than $5, tobacco, or liquor.

Canadian Customs Exemptions for returning Canadians range from $20 to $300, depending on your length of stay out of the country. For the $300 exemption, you must have been out of the country for one week. In any given year, you are allowed only one $300 exemption. You may bring in duty-free up to 50 cigars, 200 cigarettes, 2.2 pounds of tobacco, and 40 ounces of liquor, provided they are declared in writing to Customs on arrival and accompany you in hand or are checked through baggage. Personal gifts that are mailed should be labeled "Unsolicited Gift—Value under $40." Obtain a copy of the Canadian Customs brochure, *I Declare*, for further details.

U.K. Customs Returning travelers age 17 or over may bring home: (1) 200 cigarettes or 100 cigarillos or 50 cigars or 250 grams of tobacco; (2) two liters of still table wine; (3) one liter of alcohol over 22% volume or two liters of alcohol under 22% volume (fortified or sparkling wine) or two more liters of still table wine; 4) 60 milliliters of perfume and 250 milliliters of toilet water; (5) other goods to a value of £32 but no more than 50 liters of beer or 25 mechanical lighters.

Traveling with Film

If your camera is new, shoot and develop a few rolls before leaving home. Pack some lens tissue and an extra battery for your built-in light meter. Invest about $10 in a skylight filter: It will protect the lens and reduce haze.

Film should be kept away from heat, so if you're driving in summer, don't store it in the glove compartment or on the shelf under the rear window. Put it behind the front seat on the floor, on the side opposite the exhaust pipe.

On a plane trip, never pack unprocessed film in check-in luggage; if your bags get X-rayed, say good-bye to your pictures. Always carry undeveloped film with you through security and ask to have it inspected by hand. (It helps to keep your film in a plastic bag, ready for quick inspection.) Inspectors at American airports are required by law to honor requests for hand inspection.

The newer scanning machines used in all U.S. airports are safe for anything from five to 500 scans, depending on the speed of your film. The effects are cumulative; you can put the same roll of film through several scans without worry, but after five scans you're asking for trouble.

If your film gets fogged and you want an explanation, send it to the **National Association of Photographic Manufacturers** (550 Mamaroneck Ave., Harrison, NY 10528). It will try to determine what went wrong. The service is free.

Language

Hungarian (Magyar) tends to look and sound intimidating at first because it is not an Indo-European language. Generally, older people speak some German, and many younger people speak at least rudimentary English. However, anyone in the tourist trade will speak at least one of the two languages.

Staying Healthy

If you have a health problem that may require you to buy prescription drugs, have your doctor write a prescription using the drug's generic name, as brand names vary from country to country. The **International Association for Medical Assistance to Travelers (IAMAT)** offers a list of approved physicians and clinics whose training meets British and American standards. For a list of Hungarian physicians and clinics that are part of this network, contact IAMAT (417 Center St., Lewiston, NY

14092, tel. 716/754–4883; in Canada: 40 Regal Rd., Guelph, Ontario N1K 1B5; in Europe: 57 Voirets, 1212 Grand-Lancy, Geneva, Switzerland). Membership is free.

Insurance

Travelers may seek insurance coverage in four areas: health and accident, lost luggage, trip cancellation, and flight. Your first step is to review your existing health and homeowner policies; some health insurance plans cover expenses incurred while traveling, some major medical plans cover emergency transportation, and some homeowner policies cover theft of luggage.

Health and Accident Several companies offer coverage designed to supplement existing health insurance for travelers:

Carefree Travel Insurance (Box 310, 120 Mineola Blvd., Mineola, NY 11501, tel. 516/294–0220 or 800/323–3149) provides coverage for emergency medical evacuation and accidental death and dismemberment. It also offers 24-hour medical phone advice.

International SOS Assistance (Box 11568, Philadelphia, PA 19116, tel. 215/244–1500 or 800/523–8930), a medical assistance company, provides emergency evacuation services, worldwide medical referrals, and optional medical insurance.

Travel Assistance International (1133 15th St. NW, Suite 400, Washington, DC 20005, tel. 202/331–1609 or 800/821–2828) provides emergency evacuation services and 24-hour medical referrals.

Travel Guard International, underwritten by Transamerica Occidental Life Companies (1145 Clark St., Stevens Point, WI 54481, tel. 715/345–0505 or 800/782–5151), offers reimbursement for medical expenses with no deductibles or daily limits and emergency evacuation services.

Wallach and Company, Inc. (243 Church St. NW, Suite 100D, Vienna, VA 22180, tel. 703/281–9500 or 800/237–6615) offers comprehensive medical coverage, including emergency evacuation services worldwide.

WorldCare Travel Assistance Association (1150 South Olive St., Suite T-233, Los Angeles, CA 90015, tel. 213/749–0909 or 800/666–4993) provides unlimited emergency evacuation, 24-hour medical referral, and an emergency message center.

Lost Luggage and Trip Cancellation On international flights, airlines are responsible for lost or damaged property of up to $9.07 per pound (or $20 per kilo) for checked baggage, and up to $400 per passenger for unchecked baggage. If you're carrying valuables, either take them with you on the plane, or purchase additional insurance for lost luggage. Some airlines will issue extra luggage insurance when you check in, but many do not. Insurance for lost, damaged, or stolen luggage is available through travel agents or directly through various insurance companies. Luggage-loss coverage is usually part of a comprehensive travel insurance package that includes personal accident, trip cancellation, and sometimes default and bankruptcy. Two companies that issue luggage insurance are **Tele-Trip** (Box 31685, 3201 Farnam St., Omaha, NE 68131, tel. 800/228–9792), a subsidiary of Mutual of Omaha, and **The Travelers Corporation** (Ticket and Travel

Dept., 1 Tower Square, Hartford, CT 06183, tel. 203/277–0111 or 800/243–3174). Tele-Trip operates sales booths at airports and also issues insurance through travel agents. Rates vary according to the length of the trip. The Travelers Corporation will insure checked or hand luggage at $500–$2,000 valuation per person, for a maximum of 180 days. Rates for one–five days for $500 valuation are $10; for 180 days, $85. Other companies with comprehensive policies include **Access America Inc.,** a subsidiary of Blue Cross–Blue Shield (Box 11188, Richmond, VA 23230, tel. 800/334–7525 or 800/284–8300) and **Near Services** (450 Prairie Ave., Suite 101, Calumet City, IL 60409, tel. 708/868–6700 or 800/654–6700); and **Travel Guard International** and **Carefree Travel Insurance** (*see* Health and Accident Insurance, *above*).

Before you go, itemize the contents of each bag in case you need to file an insurance claim. Be certain to put your home or business address on each piece of luggage, including carry-on bags. If your lost or stolen luggage is later recovered, the airline will deliver it to your home free of charge.

Flight Flight insurance is often included in the price of a ticket when paid for with American Express, Visa, and other major credit cards. It is usually included in combination travel insurance packages available from most tour operators, travel agents, and insurance agents.

Car Rentals

There are no special requirements for renting a car in Hungary, but be sure to shop around, as prices can differ greatly. **Avis** and **Hertz** offer Western makes for as much as $400–$900 per week. Smaller local companies, on the other hand, can rent Hungarian cars for as low as $130 per week.

The following companies have offices at Budapest airport:

Avis/IBUSZ, tel. 361/1475–574 or 800/331–1212.
Budget/Coop-Car, tel. 361/1477–328 or 800/527–0700.
Europcar/Volántourist, Terminal 1, tel. 361/1342–540; Terminal 2, tel. 361/1578–519 or 800/227–7368.
Hertz/Fötaxi, tel. 361/1579–123 or 800/654–3131.

Rail Passes

The **EurailPass,** valid for unlimited first-class train travel through 17 countries, including Hungary, is an excellent value if you plan to travel around the Continent. The ticket is available for periods of 15 days ($390), 21 days ($498), one month ($616), two months ($840), and three months ($1,042). For two or more people traveling together, a 15-day rail pass costs $298. Between April 1 and September 30, you need a minimum of three in your group to get this discount. For those less than 26 years old, the **Eurail Youthpass** is available for one or two months of unlimited second-class train travel at $425 and $560.

For travelers who like to spread out their train journeys, there is the **Eurail Flexipass.** With the 15-day Flexipass ($230) you get five days of unlimited first-class travel that can be spread out over 15 days; a 21-day pass gives you 9 days of unlimited first-class travel ($398), and a one-month pass gives you 14 days ($498).

The EurailPass is available only if you live outside Europe or North Africa. You can apply through an authorized travel agent or through **Rail Europe** (610 5th Ave., New York, NY 10020, tel. 800/345–1990).

The **European East Pass** is good for unlimited first-class travel on the national railroads of Austria, Czechoslovakia, Hungary, and Poland. The Flexipass ($160) allows five days of travel within a 15-day period or 10 days of travel within 30 days ($259). Apply through your travel agent or through Rail Europe (*see above*).

Student and Youth Travel

The **International Student Identity Card** (ISIC) entitles students to special fares on local transportation, rail passes, intra-European student charter flights, and discounts at museums, theaters, sports events, and many other attractions. If the ISIC card is purchased in the United States, the $14 cost also includes $3,000 in emergency medical coverage plus hospital coverage of $100 a day for up to 60 days. Apply to the **Council on International Educational Exchange (CIEE)** (205 E. 42nd St., New York, NY 10017, tel. 212/661–1414). In Canada, the ISIC is available for $12 (Canadian) from Travel Cuts (187 College St., Toronto, Ont. M5T 1P7, tel. 416/979–2406). In the United Kingdom students enrolled in university programs can purchase the ISIC at any student's union or student travel company upon presentation of of a valid university ID.

Travelers (students and nonstudents) under 26 can apply for a **Youth International Educational Exchange Card (YIEE)** issued by the Federation of International Youth Travel Organizations (FIYTO, 81 Islands Brugge, DK-2300 Copenhagen S, Denmark). Its services and benefits are similar to those provided by the ISIC; it is available in the United States from CIEE (address above) or from ISE (Europa House, 802 W. Oregon St., Urbana, IL 61801, tel. 217/344–5863). In Canada contact the **Canadian Hostelling Association (CHA)** (1600 James Naismith Drive, Suite 608, Gloucester, Ont. K1B 5N4, tel. 613/748–5638).

An **International Youth Hostel Federation (IYHF)** membership card is the key to inexpensive dormitory-style accommodations at more than 5,000 hostel locations in 68 countries around the world. Hostels provide separate sleeping quarters for men and women at rates ranging from $7 to $20 a night per person, and many have family accommodations. Youth Hostel memberships, which are valid for 12 months from the time of purchase, are available in the United States through **American Youth Hostels (AYH)** (Box 37613, Washington, DC 20013, tel. 202/783–6161), in Canada through the **Canadian Hostelling Association** (*see above*), and in the United Kingdom through the **Youth Hostel Association of England and Wales** (Trevelyan House, 8 St. Stephen's Hill, St. Albans, Herts AL1 2DY, tel. 0727/55215). By joining one of the national (American, Canadian, or British) youth hostel associations, members automatically become part of the International Youth Hostel Federation and are entitled to special reductions on rail and bus travel around the world. Handbooks listing these special concessions are available from the associations. The cost for a first-year membership is $25 for adults 18–54; renewal thereafter is $15. For youths (17 and under) the rate is $10; and for senior citizens (55 and older) the rate is $15. Family membership is available for $35.

Economical bicycle tours for small groups of adventurous, energetic students are a popular AYH student travel service. For information on these and other AYH activities and publications, contact AYH at the address above.

Council Travel, a CIEE subsidiary, is the foremost U.S. student travel agency, specializing in low-cost charters and serving as the exclusive U.S. agent for many student airfare bargains and tours. CIEE's 80-page *Student Travel Catalog* and Council Charter brochures are available free from any Council Travel office in the United States (enclose $1 postage if ordering by mail). In addition to CIEE headquarters at 205 East 42nd Street (tel. 212/661–1450) and branch office at 35 West 8th Street in New York City, Council Travel has offices in California (Berkeley, La Jolla, Long Beach, Los Angeles, San Diego, San Francisco, and Sherman Oaks); Colorado (Boulder); Connecticut (New Haven); Washington, DC; Georgia (Atlanta); Illinois (Chicago, Evanston); Louisiana (New Orleans); Massachusetts (Amherst, Boston, Cambridge); Minnesota (Minneapolis); North Carolina (Durham); Oregon (Portland); Rhode Island (Providence); Texas (Austin, Dallas); Washington (Seattle); and Wisconsin (Milwaukee).

The **Educational Travel Center** (438 N. Frances St., Madison, WI 53703, tel. 608/256–5551) is another student-travel specialist worth contacting for information on tours, bargain fares, and bookings.

Students who would like to work abroad should contact CIEE's **Work Abroad Department** (205 E. 42nd St., New York, NY 10017, tel. 212/661–1414, ext. 1130). The council arranges paid and voluntary work experiences overseas for up to six months. CIEE also sponsors study programs in Europe, Latin America, Asia, and Australia and produces several books of interest to the student traveler. These include *Work, Study, Travel Abroad: The Whole World Handbook* ($10.95 plus $1 book-rate postage or $2.50 first-class postage); *Volunteer! The Comprehensive Guide to Voluntary Service in the U.S. and Abroad* ($6.95 plus $1 book-rate postage or $2.50 first-class postage); and *The Teenager's Guide to Travel, Study, and Adventure Abroad* ($9.95 plus $1 book-rate postage or $2.50 first-class postage).

The **Information Center** at the **Institute of International Education (IIE)** (809 U.N. Plaza, New York, NY 10017, tel. 212/984–5413) has reference books, foreign-university catalogues, study-abroad brochures, and other materials that may be consulted free of charge. The Information Center is open weekdays 10–4 and is closed on holidays.

Students visiting Hungary may also want to contact the **Express Youth and Students Travel Office** (H-1052, Budapest, Semmelweis utca 4, tel. 1176–6634), which offers information on student travel throughout the country. The brochure *Budapest—A Practical Guide for Young People,* available from both IBUSZ and the Hungarian Tourist Board, includes information on low-cost accommodations in the city, student restaurants, transportation, and cultural attractions. Students with an

ISIC or other student identification are also entitled to free or half-price admission to all museums.

Traveling with Children

Publications *Family Travel Times* is a newsletter published 10 times a year by TWYCH (Travel with Your Children, 80 Eighth Ave., New York, NY 10011, tel. 212/206–0688). A one-year subscription costs $35 and includes access to back issues. The organization also offers a free phone-in service with advice and information on specific destinations.

Great Vacations with Your Kids, by Dorothy Jordan and Marjorie Cohen, offers complete advice on planning your trip with children, from toddlers to teens ($12.95 paperback, E.P. Dutton, 375 Hudson St., New York, NY 10014, tel. 212/366–2000).

Kids and Teens in Flight, a useful brochure about flying alone, is available from the U.S. Department of Transportation. To order a free copy, call 202/366–2220.

Innocents Abroad: Traveling with Kids in Europe, by Valerie Wolf Deutsch and Laura Sutherland, is a new guide to child- and teen-friendly activities, food, and transportation on the Continent, with individual sections on each country ($14.95 paperback, New American Library, Penguin USA, 375 Hudson St., New York, NY 10014, tel. 212/366–2000).

The Adventures of Mickey, Taggy, Puppo, and Cica and How They Discover Budapest, by Kati Rekai (Canadian Stage and Arts Publications, Toronto), is an animal fantasy for children, set in Budapest and written by a Hungarian-born author.

Getting There All children, including infants, must have a valid passport for foreign travel; family passports are no longer issued. On international flights, children under two not occupying a seat pay 10% of the adult fare. Various discounts apply to children from ages 2 to 12, so check with your airline when making reservations.

Regulations about infant travel on airplanes are in the process of changing, so to be sure your infant is secure, you must bring your own infant car seat and buy a separate ticket. Check with the airline in advance so that your seat will meet the required standard. If possible, reserve a seat behind one of the plane's bulkheads, where there's usually more legroom and enough space to fit a bassinet (which is available from the airlines). The booklet *Child/Infant Safety Seats Acceptable for Use in Aircraft* is available from the Federal Aviation Administration (APA-200, 800 Independence Ave. SW, Washington, DC 20591, tel. 202/267–3479). If you opt to hold your baby on your lap, do so with the infant outside the seatbelt rather than inside it.

When reserving tickets, ask about special children's meals or snacks. The February 1990 and 1992 issues of *Family Travel Times* include TWYCH's airline guide, which contains a rundown of the children's services offered by 46 airlines.

Hotels The **Budapest Hilton** (tel. 800/445–8667) offers a "Family Plan," allowing children of all ages to stay free in their parents' room. Both the **InterContinental** and the **Forum** hotels in Budapest (tel. 800/327–0200) allow one child under 13 to stay free in his parents' room. If a rollaway bed is needed, there is a nominal charge.

Baby-sitting Inquire at the Tourinform bureau, or ask at the hotel desk for
Services information.

Hints for Disabled Travelers

Provisions for handicapped travelers in Eastern Europe are extremely limited, and traveling with a nondisabled companion is
probably the best solution. Many hotels, especially large
American or international chains, offer some wheelchair-acces-
sible rooms, but special facilities at museums, restaurants, and
on public transportation are difficult to come by.

In Budapest, information on special services and tours for the
disabled is available from **Piknik Tours** (Pinceszer ut 14–16,
tel. 1176–2722).

The **Information Center for Individuals with Disabilities** (Fort
Point Pl., 1st floor, 27–43 Wormwood St., Boston, MA 02210,
tel. 617/727–5540; TDD 617/727–5236) offers useful assistance,
including lists of travel agents who specialize in tours for the
disabled.

Moss Rehabilitation Hospital Travel Information Service (1200
W. Tabor Rd., Philadelphia, PA 19141, tel. 215/456–9600; TDD
215/456–9602) for a small fee provides information on tourist
sights, transportation, and accommodations in destinations
around the world. They also offer toll-free telephone numbers
of airlines that have special lines for the hard of hearing.

Travel Industry and Disabled Exchange (TIDE) (5435 Donna
Ave., Tarzana, CA 91356, tel. 818/368–5648) publishes a quar-
terly newsletter and a directory of travel agencies and tours catering specifically to the disabled. The annual membership fee
is $15.

Mobility International USA (Box 3551, Eugene, OR 97403, tel.
503/343–1284—voice and TDD) is an internationally affiliated
organization with 500 members. It coordinates exchange programs for disabled people around the world and offers information on accommodations and organized study programs. The
annual fee is $20.

The Society for the Advancement of Travel for the Handicapped
(26 Court St., Penthouse Suite, Brooklyn, NY 11242, tel. 718/
858–5483) provides access information and lists of tour operators specializing in travel for the disabled. Annual membership
costs $45, or $25 for students and senior citizens. Send $1 and a
stamped, self-addressed envelope for information on a specific
destination.

Publications *The Itinerary* (Box 2012, Bayonne, NJ 07002, tel. 201/858–
3400) is a bimonthly travel magazine for the disabled. Call for a
subscription ($10 for one year, $20 for two); it's not available in
bookstores.

Access to the World: A Travel Guide for the Handicapped, by
Louise Weiss, offers tips on travel and accessibility around the
world. It is available from Henry Holt & Co. for $12.95 (tel.
800/247–3912; the order number is 0805–001417).

Twin Peaks Press (Box 129, Vancouver, WA 98666, tel. 206/694–
2462 or 800/637–2256 for orders only) specializes in books for
the disabled. *Travel for the Disabled* offers helpful hints as well
as a comprehensive list of guidebooks and facilities geared to

the disabled. The *Directory of Travel Agencies for the Disabled* lists more than 350 agencies throughout the world. Twin Peaks also offers the Traveling Nurse's Network, which provides registered nurses to accompany and assist disabled travelers.

Hints for Older Travelers

The **American Association of Retired Persons (AARP)** (1909 K St. NW, Washington, DC 20049, tel. 202/662–4850) has two programs for independent travelers. The Purchase Privilege Program offers discounts on hotels, airfare, car rentals, RV rentals, and sightseeing. The AARP Motoring Plan, provided by Amoco, furnishes emergency road-service aid and trip routing information for an annual fee of $33.95 per person or couple. The AARP also arranges group tours, cruises, and apartment living in Europe and Australia through AARP Travel Experience from American Express (Box 5850, Norcross, GA 30091, tel. 800/927–0111). AARP members must be 50 years or older; annual dues are $5 per person or couple.

If you're allowed to use an AARP or other senior-citizen identification card to obtain a reduced hotel rate, mention it when you make your reservation, rather than when you check out. At participating restaurants, show your card to the maître d' before you're seated, because discounts may be limited to certain menus, days, or hours. When renting a car, be sure to ask about special promotional rates, which might offer greater savings than the available discount.

Elderhostel (75 Federal St., 3rd floor, Boston, MA 02110, tel. 617/426–7788) is an innovative educational program for people 60 and older. Participants live in dorms on some 1,200 campuses around the world. Mornings are devoted to lectures and seminars; afternoons, to sightseeing and field trips. Fees for two- to three-week trips—including room, board, tuition, and round-trip transportation—range from $1,800 to $4,500.

Mature Outlook (6001 N. Clark St., Chicago, IL 60660, tel. 800/336–6330), a subsidiary of Sears, Roebuck & Co., is a travel club for people over 50 that provides hotel and motel discounts and publishes a bimonthly newsletter. Annual membership is $9.95; there are currently 800,000 members. Instant membership is available at Sears stores and participating Holiday Inns.

National Council of Senior Citizens (925 15th St. NW, Washington, DC 20005, tel. 202/347–8800) is a nonprofit advocacy group with some 5,000 local clubs across the United States. Annual membership is $12 per person or couple. Members receive a monthly newspaper with travel information and an ID card for reduced-rate hotels and car rentals.

Saga International Holidays (120 Boylston St., Boston, MA 02116, tel. 800/343–0273) specializes in group travel for people over 60. A selection of variously priced tours allows you to choose the package that meets your needs.

Publications The *International Health Guide for Senior Citizen Travelers*, by W. Robert Lange, M.D., is available for $4.95 plus $1 for shipping, from Pilot Books (103 Cooper St., Babylon, NY 11702, tel. 516/422–2225).

The *Discount Guide for Travelers Over 55,* by Caroline and Walter Weintz, lists helpful addresses, package tours, and reduced-rate car rentals in the United States and abroad. Send $7.95 plus $1.50 shipping and handling to NAL/Cash Sales (Bergenfield Order Dept., 120 Woodbine St., Bergenfield, NJ 07621, tel. 800/526–0275).

Arriving and Departing

From North America by Plane

There are three types of flights: nonstop (no changes, no stops); direct (no changes but one or more stops); and connecting (two or more planes, one or more stops).

Airports and Airlines
Hungary's international airport, **Ferihegy Airport** in Budapest (the nation's only commercial airport), is about 22 kilometers (14 miles) southeast of the city. All **Malév** flights (except Paris flights) operate from the new Terminal 2 (tel. 1577–831). Although it's 4 kilometers (2.5 miles) farther from the city, its streamlined facilities and ground transportation make it well worth the extra time and travel costs involved in coordinating your schedule to a Malév flight. The European airlines fly into Terminal 1 (tel. 1572–122). For same-day flight information, tel. 1577–155. Malév and other national airlines fly nonstop from most European capitals.

British Airways, tel. 361/1183–299, 361/1183–041; at airport tel. 361/1579–123, ext. 8380; 800/247–9297.

Malév, tel. 361/1184–333, 361/1172–911; airport tel. 361/1579–123.

Flying Time
From New York, a nonstop flight to Budapest takes 9–10 hours; with a stopover, the journey will take at least 12–13 hours.

Enjoying the Flight
If you're lucky enough to be able to sleep on a plane, it makes sense to fly at night. Because the air on a plane is dry, it helps to drink a lot of nonalcoholic beverages; drinking alcohol contributes to jet lag, as does eating heavy meals on board. Feet swell at high altitudes, so it's a good idea to remove your shoes at the beginning of your flight. Sleepers usually prefer window seats to curl up against; those who like to move around the cabin ask for aisle seats. Bulkhead seats (located in the front row of each cabin) have more legroom, but trays are attached rather awkwardly to the arms of the seat rather than to the back of the seat ahead. Bulkhead seats are reserved for the disabled, the elderly, or parents traveling with babies.

Discount Flights
The major airlines offer a range of tickets that can increase the price of any given seat by more than 300%, depending on the day of purchase. As a rule, the further in advance you buy the ticket, the less expensive it is but the greater the penalty (up to 100%) for canceling. Check with airlines for details.

The best buy is not necessarily an APEX (advance purchase) ticket on one of the major airlines, because these tickets carry certain restrictions. They must be bought in advance (usually 21 days); they restrict your travel, usually with a minimum stay of seven days and a maximum of 90; and they also penalize you for changes—voluntary or not—in your travel plans. But if you can work around these drawbacks (and most travelers can), they are among the best-value fares available.

Travelers willing to put up with some restrictions and inconveniences, in exchange for a substantially reduced airfare, may be interested in flying as an air courier. A person who agrees to be a courier must accompany shipments between designated points. For a telephone directory that lists courier companies by the cities to which they fly, send $5 and a self-addressed, stamped, business-size envelope to Pacific Data Sales Publishing, 2554 Lincoln Blvd., Suite 275-I, Marina Del Rey, CA 90291). For "A Simple Guide to Courier Travel" send $15.95 (includes postage and handling) to Guide, Box 2394, Lake Oswego, OR 97035. For more information, call 800/344–9375.

Charter flights offer the lowest fares but often depart only on certain days and seldom on time. Though you may be able to arrive at one city and return from another, you may lose all or most of your money if you cancel your trip. Don't sign up for a charter flight until you've checked the packager's reputation with a travel agency. It's particularly important to know the packager's policy concerning refunds for a canceled flight; some travel agents recommend that travelers purchase trip-cancellation insurance if they plan to book charter flights.

Somewhat more expensive, but up to 50% below the cost of APEX fares are tickets purchased through consolidators, companies that buy blocks of tickets on scheduled airlines and sell them at wholesale prices. Tickets are subject to availability, so passengers must generally have flexible travel schedules. Here again, you may lose all or most of your money if you change plans, but at least you will be on a regularly scheduled flight with less risk of cancellation than on a charter. As an added precaution, you may want to purchase trip-cancellation insurance. Once you've made your reservation, call the airline to confirm it. **UniTravel** (Box 12485, St. Louis, MO 63132, tel. 314/569–2501 or 800/325–2222) is a well-known consolidator that offers discount tickets to Eastern Europe. Others advertise in the Sunday travel section of newspapers.

Another option is to join a travel club that offers special discounts to its members. Several such organizations are **Discount Travel International** (114 Forrest Ave., Narberth, PA 19072, tel. 215/668–7184); **Moment's Notice** (425 Madison Ave., New York, NY 10017, tel. 212/486–0503); **Travelers Advantage** (CUC Travel Service, 49 Music Square W., Nashville, TN 37203, tel. 800/548–1116); and **Worldwide Discount Travel Club** (1674 Meridian Ave., Miami Beach, FL 33139, tel. 305/534–2082). These cut-rate tickets should be compared with APEX tickets on the major airlines.

Smoking   If cigarette smoke bothers you, ask for a seat far from the smoking section. It is best to request a nonsmoking seat when you book your ticket. If a U.S. airline representative tells you there are no seats available in the nonsmoking section, insist on one: Department of Transportation regulations require U.S. flag carriers to find seats for all nonsmokers on the day of the flight, provided they meet check-in time restrictions.

From the United Kingdom by Plane, Car, and Train

By Plane   **British Airways** (tel. 071/897–4000) and **Malév Hungarian Airlines** offer daily nonstop service to Budapest from London (with connections to major British cities).

By Car The best ferry ports for Budapest are Hoek van Hooland or Oostende, from which you drive to Cologne (Köln) then through Munich to Vienna and on to Budapest.

By Train To travel from London to Budapest by train, make a reservation (required) on the **Oostende-Wien Express,** which provides convenient all-year service from Oostende. Connecting trains leave London's Victoria Station every day at 9 PM for Dover and Oostende (in summer you can leave Victoria Station at noon if you take the fast Jetfoil service). The train runs via Brussels and Cologne to Vienna (West), which it reaches in good time to change to the **Wiener Walzer,** which makes the final leg of the trip of Budapest. (The *Wiener Walzer* connects Basel, Switzerland, with Budapest, running via Zürich, Salzburg, and Vienna; reservations are required.)

Staying in Hungary

Getting Around

By Train Travel by train from Budapest to other large cities or to Lake Balaton is cheap and efficient. Remember to take *gyorsvonat* (express trains) and not *személyvonat* (locals), which are extremely slow. A *helyjegy* (seat reservation), which costs 16 Ft. and is sold up to 60 days in advance, is advisable for all express trains, especially during weekend travel in summer. It is also worth paying a little extra for first-class tickets.

Fares Unlimited-travel tickets for 7 or 10 days are inexpensive— 1,400 Ft. and 2,000 Ft., respectively (subject to change). All students with a valid ID receive 50% off. InterRail cards are valid for those under 26, and the Rail Europe Senior Travel Pass entitles senior citizens to a 30% reduction on all trains. Snacks and drinks are available on all express trains, but the supply often runs out quickly, especially in summer, so pack a lunch just in case. For more information about rail travel, contact or visit **MAV Passenger Service,** Andrassy útja 35, Budapest VI (tel. 361/1228–049).

By Bus Long-distance buses link Budapest with most cities in Hungary as well as with much of Eastern and Western Europe. Services to the eastern part of the country leave from Nepstadion station (tel. 361/1187–315). Buses to the west and south, to Austria and Yugoslavia, leave from the main Volan bus station at Erzsebet tér in downtown Pest (tel. 361/1172–966). Although inexpensive, they tend to be crowded, so reserve your seat.

By Boat Hungary is well equipped with nautical transport, and Budapest is situated on a major international waterway, the Danube. Vienna is five hours away by hydrofoil or boat. For information about excursions or pleasure cruises, contact **MAHART Landing Stage** (Vigadó tér 1, Budapest V, tel. 361/1181–223) or **IBUSZ** (Hungarian Travel Bureau) (Tanács körút 3/C, Budapest VII, tel. 361/1423–140 or 361/1211–007).

By Car To drive in Hungary, U.S. and Canadian visitors need an Inter-
Documentation national Driver's License, and U.K. visitors need a domestic driving license.

Road Conditions There are three classes of roads: highways (designated by the letter M and a single digit), secondary roads (designated by a two-digit number), and minor roads (designated by a three-digit number). Highways and secondary roads are generally excellent; the condition of minor roads varies considerably. There are no toll charges on highways.

Rules of the Road Hungarians drive on the right and observe the usual Continental rules of the road. The speed limit in developed areas is 60 kph (37 mph), on main roads 80 kph (50 mph), and on highways 120 kph (75 mph). Seat belts are compulsory and drinking is strictly prohibited, with very servere penalties.

Gasoline Gas stations are not as plentiful in Hungary as in Western Europe, so fill up whenever possible and check on tourist maps for the exact location of stations throughout the country. A gallon of gasoline *(benzin)* costs about $3.50. Unleaded gasoline, only slightly more expensive, is available in Budapest, on all the major routes from the city, and at a growing number of stations in the provinces. Interag Shell and Afor stations at busy traffic centers stay open all night; elsewhere, from 6 AM to 8 PM. Diesel oil can be bought only with coupons from IBUSZ travel offices at the border or from hotels. They are nonrefundable, so try to estimate how many you will need.

Breakdowns The **Hungarian Automobile Club** runs a 24-hour "Yellow Angels" breakdown service from Budapest XIV (Frácia út 38/A, tel. 361/1691–831 or 361/1693–714). There are repair stations in all the major towns with emergency telephones on the main highways.

By Bicycle A land of rolling hills and flat plains, Hungary lends itself to bicycling. The larger train stations around Lake Balaton have bicycles for rent at about 100 Ft. a day. For information about renting bicycles in Budapest, contact **Tourinform** (Šutő utca 2, tel. 361/1179–800). **HUNTOURS** provides full service for guided bicycle tours (Retek utca 34, tel. 361/1152–403).

Telephones

Local Calls Pay phones use 5-Ft. coins—the cost of a three-minute local call. Most towns in Hungary can be called directly; dial 06, wait for the buzzing tone, then dial the local number.

International Calls Direct calls to foreign countries can be made from Budapest and all major provincial towns, but only by using the red push-button telephones; or from hotels and post offices, by dialing 00 and waiting for the international dialing tone. The phones take 5-, 10-, and 20-Ft. coins.

Operators International calls can be made through the operator by dialing 09; for operator-assisted calls within Hungary dial 01. Dial tel. 361/1172–200 for information in English. The entire telephone system is currently being updated.

Mail

Postal Rates An airmail postcard to the United States, the United Kingdom, and the rest of Western Europe costs 18 Ft., and postage for an airmail letter starts at 24 Ft. Postcards to the United Kingdom and the rest of Western Europe cost 10 Ft., letters, 15 Ft. Stamps can be bought at tobacco shops as well as post offices. The post offices at the Keleti (East) and Nyugati (West) train stations in Budapest are open 24 hours.

Receiving Mail A poste restante service is available in Budapest. The address is Magyar Posta, H-1052 Budapest, Petőfi Sándor utca 17–19.

Tipping

Four decades of socialism have not restrained the extended palm in Hungary—so when in doubt, tip. Cloakroom and gas-pump attendants, hairdressers, waiters, and taxi drivers all expect tips. Although hotel bills include a service charge, you should also tip the elevator operator, chambermaid, and head porter; together, they should get 10% of the bill. At least an extra 10% should be added to a restaurant bill or taxi fare. If a Gypsy band plays exclusively for your table, you can leave 100 Ft. in a plate discreetly provided for that purpose.

Opening and Closing Times

Banks are open weekdays 8–1. Most **museums** are open daily from 10 to 6 and are closed on Mondays. **Shops** are open weekdays 10–6, Saturday 9–1; many shops stay open until 8 on Thursday.

National Holidays January 1; March 15 (Anniversary of 1848 revolution); April 19 and 20 (Easter and Easter Monday); May 1 (Labor Day); August 20 (St. Stephen's and Constitution Day); October 23 (1956 Revolution Day); December 25 and 26.

Shopping

The best buys in Hungary are peasant embroideries and the exquisite Herend and Zsolnay porcelain. Hand-painted pottery and handmade lace are also attractive, as is the excellent cut glass. Dolls dressed in national costume are popular, and phonograph records are of good quality and inexpensive.

Government tourist shops, called *Intertourist* or *Konsumtourist*, have multilingual assistants and stock the widest choice. They sell only against convertible currency.

Sports and Outdoor Activities

Golf There is a golf course in the small village of **Kisoroszi,** about 38 kilometers (23 miles) from Budapest. The course has nine holes, which will be increased to 18. The clubhouse has a restaurant and sports store, and equipment can be rented. Make reservations through the Budapest Hilton, tel. 361/1751–000.

Horseback Riding Traditionally a nation of horsemen, Hungary has more than 100 riding schools and stables. They range from small holdings with two or three horses to large establishments with 50 to 60 horses and comfortable guest houses. Among the many options available are one-day outings, 10-day tours covering up to 250 kilometers (155 miles), and even courses in horse-driving. Hungary is especially well suited to cross-country riders who have already acquired the basic skills. IBUSZ offices abroad will supply information and make reservations. In Budapest, TOURINFORM can answer any queries.

Water Sports Lake Balaton and the Danube are the main centers. Yachts, rowboats, and sailboards can be rented at lake resorts, and sailing courses are organized for beginners. Sailing holidays on

Lake Balaton can be arranged through IBUSZ and SIOTOUR, Budapest VII, Wesselényi utca 26.

Budapest is dotted with swimming pools, many of them attached to the medicinal baths and mineral springs. Of the many pools, the largest and finest is the Palatinus Lido on Margaret Island.

Dining

Throughout the lean postwar years, the Hungarian kitchen lost none of its spice and sparkle, particularly in restaurants favored by foreigners—for whom everything was and still is available. Consider sampling traditional dishes—goulash, paprika, cabbage, and pastries—at the breakfast buffets of the posh hotels, where leftovers are served up piping hot and still fresh. This will leave you free at lunch and dinner to explore Budapest's less familiar culinary treats, such as fiery fish soups; *fogas* (pike perch) from Lake Balaton; and goose liver, duck, and veal specialties. Portions are large, so don't expect to digest more than one main Hungarian meal a day. The desserts are lavish, and every inn seems to have its house *torta* (tart); though *rétes* (strudels), *Somlói galuska* (a steamed sponge cake soaked in chocolate sauce and whipped cream), and Gundel pancakes are ubiquitous. Unless you're taking a cure in a spa, don't expect to lose weight in Hungary.

Ratings	Category	All Areas*
	Very Expensive	over 1,200 Ft.
	Expensive	1,000–1,200 Ft.
	Moderate	600–1,000 Ft.
	Inexpensive	under 600 Ft.

Prices are per person, including first course, main course, and dessert and excluding wine and tip.

Wine   **Tokay,** the best-known and most prolific white wine, can be too heavy, dark, and sweet for many tastes, even Hungarians' (which is why red wine is often recommended with poultry, veal, and even fish dishes), but **Tokaji Aszú,** the best of the breed, makes a good dessert wine. **Badacsony** white wines are lighter and livelier, though seldom dry enough for some.

The gourmet red table wine of Hungary, **Egri Bikavér** (Bull's Blood of Eger, usually with *el toro* himself on the label), is the best buy and safest bet with all foods. Other good reds and the best roses come from **Villanyi;** the most adventurous reds—with sometimes successful links to both Austrian and California wine-making and grape-growing—are from the **Sopron** area, though you can sometimes drink a red that tastes pink. Before- and after-dinner drinks tend toward schnapps, most notable **Barack-pálinka,** an apricot brandy. A plum brandy called **Kosher szilva-pálinka,** bottled under rabbinical supervision, is very chic. Hard to find, but worth the effort, is **Blauer Engel** (the label that honors Marlene Dietrich), which looks like Windex but tastes like fairly dry champagne.

Beer and Ale   Major Hungarian beers are Köbányai, Dreher, Aranyhordó, Balaton, Világos, and Aszok. Czech, German, and Austrian beers are widely available on tap.

Lodging

When it comes to hotels and hostels Budapest is modestly equipped to handle the increase in tourism since its move toward Westernization. Advance reservations are strongly advised especially at the lower-price hotels. Some hotels have large numbers of rooms reserved through booking agencies such as IBUSZ, but you can save yourself the commission if you book a room directly. If a hotel receptionist tells you no rooms are available, that means the rooms the hotel books itself all are occupied. Solo travelers are especially encouraged to make reservations to avoid an exhausting runaround. Many hotels don't have single rooms, making advance notice to those that *do* all the more important. In winter it's pretty easy to find a hotel room at the last minute, and prices are usually reduced by 20%–30%. By far the cheapest and most accessible beds in the city are rooms (400 Ft.–500 Ft. per person) in private homes. Although most tourist offices book private rooms, the supply is limited, so try to arrive in Budapest early in the morning.

There are no Very Expensive and few Expensive hotels outside Budapest. The Moderate hotels are generally comfortable and well run, although single rooms with baths are scarce. Establishments in the Inexpensive category seldom have private baths, but plumbing is adequate almost everywhere. Reservations should be made well in advance, especially at the less expensive establishments, which are still in short supply.

Rentals   Apartments in Budapest and cottages at Lake Balaton are available. Rates and reservations can be obtained from tourist offices in Hungary and abroad. A Budapest apartment might cost 10,000 Ft. a week, while a luxury cottage for two on the Balaton costs around 35,000 Ft. a week. Bookings can be made in Budapest at the **IBUSZ** on Petöfi tér 3 (tel. 361/1185–707), which is open 24 hours a day, or through IBUSZ offices in the United States and Great Britain.

Guest Houses   Also called pensions, these offer simple accommodations and rooms with four beds. They are well suited to younger people on a budget, and there are separate bathrooms for men and women on each floor. Some offer simple breakfast facilities. Arrangements can be made through local tourist offices or travel agents abroad.

In the provinces it is safe to accept rooms that you are offered directly. *Szoba kiadó* (or the German *Zimmer frei*) means "room to rent." The rate per night for a double room in Budapest or at Lake Balaton is around 1,200 Ft., which includes the use of a bathroom but not breakfast. If you prefer, reservations can also be made through any tourist office.

Camping   The 140 campsites in Hungary are open from May through September. Rates are 300–400 Ft. a day. With a small charge for hot water and electricity plus an accommodations fee of 25–75 Ft. per person per night. Children get a 50% reduction. Camping is forbidden except in appointed areas. Reservations can be made through travel agencies or through the **Hungarian Camp-**

ing and Caravanning Club (Budapest IX, Kálvin tér 9, tel. 361/
1177–208).

Ratings The following price categories are for a double room with bath
and breakfast during the peak season. For single rooms with
bath, count on about 80% of the double-room rate. Prices are
quoted in forints.

Category	Budapest	Balaton	Provinces
Very Expensive	9,000–14,000	7,000–12,000	6,000–10,000
Expensive	7,000–9,000	6,000–7,000	3,500–6,000
Moderate	4,000–7,000	3,500–6,000	2,500–3,500
Inexpensive	1,500–4,000	1,200–3,500	800–2,500

During the peak season (June through August), full board may
be compulsory at the Lake Balaton hotels. During the off-sea-
son (in Budapest, September through March; at Lake Balaton,
May and September), rates can be considerably lower than
those given above.

Credit Cards

The following credit card abbreviations are used: AE, American Express; D, Discover; DC, Diners Club; MC, MasterCard/
Access/Barclay's; V, Visa.

2 Budapest

Essential Information

Important Addresses and Numbers

Tourist Information
Tourinform (Sütö utca 2, tel. 361/1179–800) is open daily 8–8. **IBUSZ Accommodation Office** (Petöfi tér 3, tel. 361/1185–707) is open 24 hours. In addition to these two official agencies, the following private offices can also provide valuable assistance: **Budapest Tourist** (Roosevelt tér 5, tel. 361/1173–555), **Taverna Tourist Service** (Váci utca 20, tel. 361/1181–818), and **American Express Travel Related Services** (V, Deák Ferenc utca 10, tel. 361/1374–394, 361/2510–010, or 361/2515–500; fax 361/2515–220).

Embassies
U.S. (Budapest V, Szabadság tér 12, tel. 361/1126–450). **Canadian** (Budapest II, Budakeszi út 32, tel. 361/1767–711). **U.K.** (Budapest V, Harmincad utca 6, tel. 361/1182–555).

Emergencies
Police (tel. 07)

Medical
Ambulance (tel. 04); **Central State Hospital** (Kutvolgyi út 4, tel. 361/1551–122).

Doctor: Ask your hotel or embassy to recommend one. U.S. and Canadian visitors are advised to take out full medical insurance. U.K. visitors are covered for emergencies and essential treatment.

Belgyogyaszati Klinika (General Clinic; Koranyi utca 2/a, tel. 361/133–0360) offers 24-hour medical service.

Stomatológiai Intézet (Central Dental Institutes; Szentkirályi utca 40, tel. 361/1330–970; Mária utca 52, tel. 361/1330–189) offers 24-hour dental services. **Buzna** (Lenin körút 73, tel. 361/111–100) is a private dental clinic.

Where to Change Money
Every major hotel will change hard currency into Hungarian forints. You can also exchange money at all banks (most are open 9 AM–2:30 PM), nearly all travel agencies (including IBUSZ travel agency offices), and at official exchange offices at border entrances.

English-language Bookstores
Foreign-Language Book Store, Budapest V, Váci utca 32. Foreign publications—including those in English—can be bought at the reception desks of major hotels and at newsstands at major traffic centers.

English-language Radio
News programs are broadcast on Radio Petöfi (1341 AM) daily at about noon; sometimes on Radio Danubius (103.3 FM) at 1 PM daily from April 15 to November 1. **Radio Bridge** on 102.1 MHz FM carries some Voice of America news and music (tel. 361/1761–019 or 361/1761–250).

Late-night Pharmacies
The state-run Pharmacies close at 8 PM, but one pharmacy in each of Budapest's 22 districts stays open at night and on the weekend. They take turns, but pharmacies post the addresses of the nearest ones open in their doorways.

Lost and Found
Before you despair, try calling the **Talált Tárgyak Központi Hivatala** (Municipal Lost Property Service) (V Erzsébet tér 5, tel. 361/1174–961). For things lost on the public transportation system, contact **BKV Talált Tárgyak Osztálya** (VII Akácfa utca 18, tel. 361/1226–613; open Mon., Tues., Thurs., and Fri. 7:30–3:30, Wed. 7:30–7); for things lost on a Danube ship, **MAHART**

(V Belgrád rakpart, tel. 361/1181–704); for things lost on a train, **Nyugati Pályaudvar** (tel. 361/1225–615); and for things lost on an airplane, **MALEV** (tel. 361/1472–784 or 361/1578–108).

Arriving and Departing by Plane

Ferihegy Airport, Hungary's only commercial airport, is about 22 kilometers (14 miles) southeast of Budapest. All **Malév** flights (except Paris flights) operate from the new Terminal 2 (tel. 361/1577–831); other airlines use Terminal 1 (tel. 361/1572–122). For same-day flight information, tel. 361/1577–155.

Between the Airport and City Center Most hotels offer their guests car or minibus transportation to and from Ferihegy, but all of them charge for the service. You should arrange for a pickup in advance.

By Taxi Allow 40 minutes in nonpeak hours and at least an hour at rush hours (7 AM–9 AM from the airport, 4 PM–6 PM from the city). A taxi ride to the center of Budapest should cost no more than 800 Ft. with tip. Avoid taxi drivers who offer their services before you are out of the arrivals lounge.

By Bus Yellow Volanbuszes run every half hour from 5 AM to 9 PM to and from the Erzsébet (formerly Engels) tér bus station in downtown Budapest in almost the same time as taxis. Cost: 100 Ft. to either terminal.

Arriving and Departing by Car, Train, Boat, and Bus

By Car The main routes into Budapest are the M1 from Vienna (via Győr) and the M7 from the Balaton.

By Train There are three main train stations in Budapest: **Keleti** (East), **Nyugati** (West), and **Déli** (South). Trains from Vienna usually operate from the Keleti station, while those to the Balaton depart from the Déli.

The fastest train from Vienna is the **Lehar**, an early-morning EuroCity express (with a small surcharge that includes a seat reservation) that makes the 160-mile run in just under three hours. Later EuroCity expresses, the afternoon **Bartole** (coming from Munich) and the **Liszt** (coming from Frankfurt and German points north), take an hour longer. Cost: 396 AS (first class), 264 AS (second class). Trains passing through Vienna to Budapest include the **Orient Express** (the slightly creaky original, not the luxurious charter special) from Paris and Stuttgart; and the **Wiener Walzer** from Basel and Zurich. Both have comfortable sleepers for their overnight runs. The **Oostende-Vienna Express** (from Brussels, Cologne, Bonn, and Frankfurt, with a Channel connection from London via Dover) has a through car that is hitched onto the Wiener Walzer in Vienna. For information in Vienna, tel. 0222/431–1717; in Budapest, tel. 361/1224–052.

By Boat From June to mid-September, two swift hydrofoils leave Vienna daily at 8 AM and 2:30 PM (once-a-day trips are scheduled in April, May, September, and October). After a 4- to 4½-hour journey downriver, with views of the Slovak capital, Bratislava, and of Hungary's largest church, the cathedral in Esztergom along the way, the boats make a grand entrance into Budapest via its main artery, the Danube. The upriver journey takes an hour longer. For reservations and information in Vienna, tel. 0222/431–21–75–00; in Budapest, tel. 361/1181–953. Cost: 79 AS one-way.

By Bus Most buses to Budapest from the western region of Hungary, including those from Vienna, arrive at Erzsebét tér station. Two deluxe buses depart daily from both Vienna and Budapest at 7 AM and 5 PM. The journey takes just under four hours. For reservations and information in Vienna, tel. 02/50180–110, in Budapest, tel. 361/1177–777. Cost: 262 AS one-way.

Getting Around

By Car Budapest, like any Western city, is plagued by traffic jams by day, but motorists have smooth sailing later in the evening. Parking, however, is a problem near any of the public housing projects.

By Subway Service on Budapest's subways is cheap, fast, frequent, and comfortable; stations are easily located on maps and streets by the big letter M (for metro) in a circle. The standard fare is 15 Ft. for any distance. Line 1 (marked Foldalatti), which starts downtown at Vorosmarty tér and follows Andrassy (formerly Nepkoztarsasag) utja out past Gundel's restaurant and the city park, is an antique tourist attraction in itself, built in the 1890's for the Magyar Millennium; its yellow trains with tank treads still work. Lines 2 and 3 were built 90 years later. Line 2 runs from the eastern suburbs, past the Keleti (East) Station, through the Inner City area, and under the Danube to the Deli (South) Station. One of the stations, Moszkva tér, is where the *Varbusz* (Castle Bus) can be boarded. Line 3 runs from the southern suburbs to Deak tér, through the Inner City, and northward to the Nyugati (West) Station and the northern suburbs. The yellow tickets (15 Ft.) used on trams are canceled in machines at the station entrance. Tickets are valid for one hour and should be kept until the end of the journey, as there are often checks by inspectors. All three metro lines meet at Deak tér station and run from 4:30 AM to 11 PM.

By Streetcar and Bus Streetcars and buses are also abundant and convenient. Blue tickets (18 Ft.) for buses and yellow tickets (15 Ft.) for the metro, tram, and HEV suburban railway can be bought at hotels, metro stations, and tobacco shops; they are canceled in the time-clock machines on board or in station entrances. There is also a one-day ticket (*Napijegy*) good for unlimited travel on all transportation services within the city limits. Fares cannot be paid on board, and there are fines for traveling without a validated ticket. Buses run from 4:30 AM and trams from 5 AM. Most lines stop operating at 11 PM, but there is all-night service on certain key lines.

By Taxi Taxis are plentiful and a good value, but make sure that they have a working meter. The initial charge is 20 Ft., with 28–30 Ft. per kilometer and 6 Ft. for each minute of waiting time. Note that these prices are only for the government-run **Volántaxi** and **Fötaxi**. Private services are more expensive. To call a taxi, tel. 1222–222 or 1666–666; to order one in advance, tel. 1188–188.

By Boat In summer a regular boat service links the north and south of the city, stopping at points on both banks, including Margitsziget (Margaret Island). From May to September boats leave from the quay at Vigado tér on 1½-hour cruises between the Árpád and Petőfi bridges. The trip, organized by MAHART, runs three times a day and costs around 200 Ft. (tel. 361/1181–223).

Guided Tours

Orientation Three-hour bus tours of the city operate year-round and cost about, 1,200 Ft. Starting from Erzsébet tér, they take in parts of both Buda and Pest and are a good introduction to further exploration on foot. Contact IBUSZ (*see* Important Addresses and Numbers, *above*).

Special-interest Tours and Excursions IBUSZ and Budapest Tourist organize a number of unusual tours, featuring trips to the Buda Hills, goulash parties, and visits to such traditional sites as the National Gallery and Parliament. These companies will provide personal guides on request. Also check at your hotel.

Excursions farther afield include daylong trips to the *Puszta* (the Great Plain), the Danube Bend, and Lake Balaton.

Boat Tours IBUSZ offers a three-hour tour on the Danube called Budapest by Boat, which includes a stop at Margaret Island, the city's pleasant park in the middle of the river. While on the island you can stroll under centuries-old chestnut trees or purchase coffee and soft drinks on the terrace of Hotel Thermal. *Departures May 1–Oct. 31, Mon., Wed., Fri., and Sun. 10 AM.*

Personal Guides The major travel agencies—**IBUSZ, Cooptourist,** and **Budapest Tourist**—will arrange for guides. The weekly English-language newspaper, *Budapest Week,* also carries advertisements for guides.

Exploring Budapest

Orientation

Budapest, bestriding both banks of the Danube, unites the colorful hills of Buda and the wide boulevards of Pest. Though the site of a Roman outpost in the first century, the modern city was not created until 1873, when the towns of Obuda, Pest, and Buda were joined. The cultural, political, intellectual, and commercial heart of the nation beats in Budapest; for the 20% of Hungary's population who live in the capital, anywhere else is simply "the country."

Much of Budapest's real charm lies in its shadowy courtyards and sunlit cobbled streets. Although some 30,000 buildings were destroyed during World War II and in the 1956 uprising, you'll find the past lingering on in the architectural details of the city's structures and in the memories and lifestyles of its residents.

The principal sights fall roughly into three areas—Buda, Pest, and Obuda—which can be comfortably covered on foot. The hills of Budapest are best explored by public transportation.

Tour 1: Castle Hill and North Buda

Numbers in the margin correspond to points of interest on the Budapest and Castle Hill (Várhegy) maps.

❶ The first destination on this tour is **Várhegy** (Castle Hill), a long, narrow plateau banned to private cars, except for those of neighborhood residents and Hilton Hotel guests. If you're already on the Buda side of the river you can take the Castle bus—*Várbusz*—from the Moszkva tér transportation hub northwest of Castle Hill. If you're starting out from Pest you can take a taxi or bus no. 16 from Erzsébet (formerly Engels) tér. Another and very scenic alternative if you're approaching from Pest is to cross the **Széchenyi lánchíd** (Chain Bridge) on foot to **Clark Ádám tér,** which is named for the bridge's builder, the Scottish engineer Adam Clark. From there you can ride up to Castle Hill on the funicular railway known as the *Sikló* (cost: 40 Ft.). Taxi, *Sikló,* and *Várbusz* will deliver you to Szent György tér (St. George Square) at the northern end of the **Királyi Palota**—Royal Palace—the first major sight on the tour of Castle Hill; bus no. 16 will leave you at Dísz tér, one block to the north.

During a seven-week siege at the end of 1944 and beginning of 1945, the entire Castle Hill district of palaces, mansions, and churches was turned into one vast ruin. The final German stand was in the Royal Palace itself, which was gutted by fire, with its walls reduced to rubble, and just a few scarred pillars and blackened statues protruding from the wreckage. The destruction was incalculable, yet it had an unanticipated advantage. It gave archaeologists and art historians a precious opportunity to explore the past, to discover the medieval buildings that once stood on the site of this Baroque and neo-Baroque palace. Details of the edifices of the kings of the Árpád and Anjou dynasties, of the Holy Roman Emperor Sigismund, and of the great 15th-century king Mátthiás Corvinus had been preserved in some 80 reports, travelogues, books, and itineraries. These spoke with the authenticity and appreciation of contemporaries about the beauty and riches of Buda's royal residence, much of which could now be restored or reconstructed.

The postwar rebuilding was slow and painstaking. In some places more than 6 meters (20 feet) of debris had to be removed, and the remains found on the medieval levels were restored to their original planes. Freed from mounds of rubble, the foundation walls and medieval castle walls were completed; and the ramparts surrounding the medieval royal residence were re-created as close to their original shape and size as possible. Out of this herculean labor emerged the Royal Palace of today, a vast museum complex and cultural center.

In front of the Palace, facing the Danube by the entrance to Wing C, stands an equestrian **Statue of Prince Eugene of Savoy,** a commander of the army that liberated Hungary from the Turks at the end of the 17th century. The hero's image has been prettified in bronze, for Eugene was a singularly ugly and unappreciated French nobleman, scorned by King Louis XIV for his ignoble appearance. The Habsburg Emperor Leopold I, however, recognized the prince's military genius and enlisted him in 1683 to turn the tide of the Turkish siege of Vienna. Eugene also eventually humbled Louis XIV at the battle of Blenheim in 1704. From the terrace on which the statue stands there is a superb view across the river to Pest.

In the Palace's northern wing (A), the **Legujabbkori Törteneti Múzeum** (Museum of Recent History), formerly the Museum of

the Hungarian Working Class Movement, hosts temporary e
hibitions and houses one of the nation's largest photo collections. *Dísz tér 17, tel. 361/175–7533. Admission: 10 Ft. adults,
5 Ft. children. Free on Sat. Open Tues.–Sun. 10–6.*

The immense center block of the Palace (made up of Wings B,
C, and D) contains the **Magyar Nemzeti Galéria** (Hungarian National Gallery), which exhibits a wide range of Hungarian fine
art, from medieval ecclesiastical paintings, stone carvings, and
statues, through Gothic, Renaissance, and Baroque art, to
works of the 19th and 20th centuries, which are richly represented. Especially notable are the works of the Romantic
painter Mihály Munkácsy (1844–1900), the Impressionist Pál
Szinyei Merse, and the neo-Surrealist Kosztka Csontváry.
There is also a large collection of modern Hungarian sculpture.
For an additional 25 Ft. groups of up to 25 can visit the **Crypt of
the Habsburg Palatines** (the ruling royal deputies) below Wing
C. *Dísz tér 17, Wings B, C, and D, tel. 361/1755–567. Admis-
sion: 20 Ft. adults, 10 Ft. children. Free on Sat. Open Apr.–
Oct., Tues.–Sun. 10–6, Nov.–Mar., Tues.–Sun. 10–4; closed
Mon.*

The Palace's Baroque southern wing (E) contains the
Budapesti Történeti Múzeum (Budapest Historic Museum),
with its permanent exhibition "Archaeological Excavations in
Budapest." Through historical documents, objects, and art it
depicts the medieval history of Buda fortress and the capital as
a whole. This is the best place to view remains of the medieval
Royal Palace and other archaeological excavations. The splen-
didly restored **Medieval Hall of the Knights** is particularly impressive. Some of the artifacts unearthed during excavations
are in the vestibule of the basement; others are still situated
among the remains of medieval structures. The Gothic statues
dating from the turn of the 14th and 15th centuries are especially significant. Some are displayed in the large Gothic Hall, others in the former lower chapel of the Palace. Down in the cellars
are the original vaults of the palace, portraits of King Mátthiás
and his second wife, Beatrice of Aragon, and many late-14th-
century statues that probably adorned the Renaissance palace.
*Szt. György tér 2, Buda Castle Palace, Wing E, tel. 361/1757–
533, ext. 253. Admission: 20 Ft. adults, 10 Ft. children. Free
on Sat. Open Apr.–Oct., Tues.–Sun. 10–6, Nov.–Mar., Tues.–
Sun. 10–4; closed Mon. Choral concerts Sun. at 11:30 (except
July–Aug.).*

The western wing of the Royal Palace is the home of the
Széchenyi National Library, which houses more than two million volumes. Its archives include well-preserved medieval codices, manuscripts, and the correspondence of historic
eminences. This is not a lending library, but the reading rooms
are open to the public, and even the most valuable incunabula
and codices can be viewed on microfilm. To arrange a tour with
an English-speaking guide, call 361/1556–967 or 361/1757–533,
ext. 384. *Open Mon.–Sat. 10–6.*

On Színház utca, a street connecting Szent György tér and Dísz
tér, the **Várszínház** (Castle Theater) was once a Franciscan
church but was transformed into a late-Baroque-style royal
theater in 1787 under the supervision of courtier Farkas
Kempelen. The first theatrical performance in Hungarian was
held here in 1790. Heavily damaged in World War II, the thea-

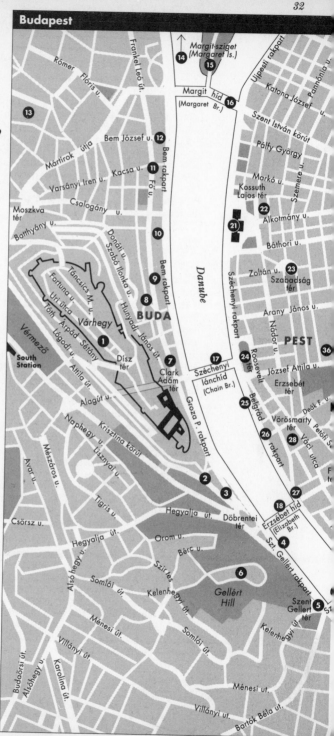

Budapest

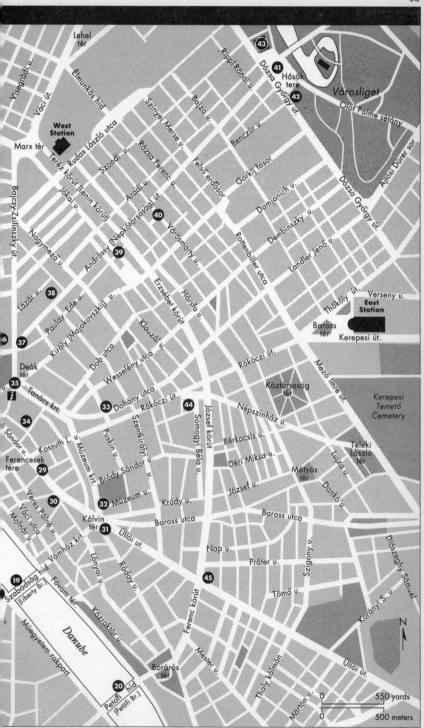

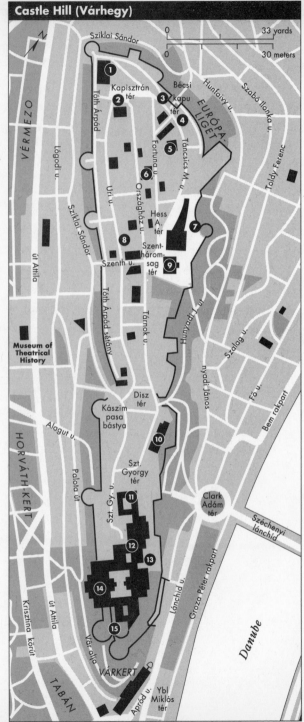

Castle Hill (Várhegy)

ter was rebuilt and reopened in 1978. While the building retains its original facade, the interior was renovated with marble and concrete. It is now used as the studio theater of the National Theater, and there is usually a historical exhibition in its foyer. *Színház utca 1–3, tel. 361/1758–011.*

From Dísz tér, two interesting streets funnel northward into **Hess András tér** and **Szentháromság (Holy Trinity) tér.** Both streets and both squares are well worth exploring. Beginning near the **Batthyány Palace** at Dísz tér 3, **Tárnok utca's** houses and usually open courtyards offer glimpses of how Hungarians have integrated contemporary life into Gothic, Renaissance, and Baroque settings; of particular interest are the houses at Nos. 7, 16 (now the Arany Hordo restaurant), and, at No. 18, the **Arany Sas Patika** (Golden Eagle Pharmacy Museum) with a naif madonna and child in an overhead niche. This tiny museum displays instruments, prescriptions, books, and other artifacts from 16th- and 17th-century pharmacies. *Tárnok utca 18, tel. 361/175–9772. Admission: 10 Ft. adults, students free. Open Tues.–Sun. 10:30–5:30; last admission at 5:30.*

Úri utca (one block to the west, parallel to Tárnok utca) has been less commercialized by boutiques and other shops; the longest and oldest street in the castle district, it is lined with many stately houses. It is worthwhile visiting the courtyard of No. 39, where you can see a 15th-century keep. On the opposite side of the street (Nos. 48–50) both gateways of the Baroque palace are articulated by Gothic niches. The **Museum of Hungarian Telephone Technology,** at No. 42, was opened in 1991. Although vintage telephone systems of museum value are still in use all over the country, both the oldest and most recent products of telecommunication can be observed and tested here, on the site of an earlier telephone exchange.

At Úri utca 9, below a house dating to the beginning of the 18th century, is the **Labyrinth of Buda Castle,** used as a wine cellar and source of water in the 16th and 17th centuries and as an air-raid shelter in World War II. Since 1984 it has housed a cave theater that presents a multimedia "War Show of the Hungarian Army" (also known as *Panoptikum*), involving marionettes and montages. At night in summer the Catacombs Restaurant and Wine Bar offers a live floor show (*see* The Arts and Nightlife, *below*). *Tel. 361/1756–858. Admission to Panoptikum show: 70 Ft. Open Tues.–Sun. 10-7; closed Mon.*

Szentháromság tér is named for its Baroque **Trinity Column,** erected in 1712–13 as a gesture of thanksgiving by survivors of a plague. The column stands in front of the Gothic **Mátyás templom** (Matthias Church), officially the Buda Church of Our Lady but better known by the name of the 15th-century's "just king" of Hungary, who was married here twice. It is sometimes called the Coronation Church because the last two kings of Hungary were crowned here: the Habsburg emperors Franz Joseph in 1867 and his grandnephew Karl IV in 1916. Originally built for the city's German population in the mid-13th century, it has endured many alterations and assaults. For almost 150 years it was the main mosque of the Turkish overlords—and the predominant impact of its festive pillars is decidedly Byzantine. Badly damaged in the recapture of Buda in 1686, it was completely rebuilt between 1873 and 1896 by Frigyes Schulek, who gave it an asymmetrical western front with one high and one low spire, and a fine rose window; the south porch is 14th-century. The paintings and sculptures are of great age and artistic value. Of particular interest in the **Trinity Chapel** is an *encolpion*—an enameled casket, containing a miniature copy of the Gospel, to be worn on the chest; it belonged to the 12th-century King Béla III and his wife, Anne of Chatillon. Their burial crowns and a cross, scepter, and rings found in their excavated graves are also displayed here. The church's **Treasury** contains Renaissance and Baroque chalices, monstrances, and vestments. High Mass is celebrated every Sunday at 10 AM with full orchestra and choir—and often with major soloists; get here early if you want a seat. In the summer there is usually an organ recital on Sunday at 8 PM. *Szentháromság tér 2. Church open Apr.– Sept. 8:30–8; Oct.–Mar. 9–7. Admission free. Admission to Treasury: 20 Ft. adults, 10 Ft. children.*

The church's wondrous porch overlooking the Danube and Pest is the neo-Romanesque **Halászbástya** (Fishermen's Bastion), a merry cluster of white stone towers and arches and columns above a modern bronze statue of St. Stephen, Hungary's first king. Medieval fishwives peddled their wares here, but it is now a mecca of souvenirs, crafts, and music. On a sunny summer morning you might hear a brass band in full uniform as well as a Hungarian zitherist sporting white handlebar mustaches and full folkloric garb, competing for your ear.

Time Out   Fishermen's Bastion is crowned by a round tower housing the **Café-Restaurant Halászbástya,** which extends along the upper rampart. It is the perfect place to watch both the distant panorama and the bastion's passing parade. *Open daily 8 AM–midnight.*

Behind Fishermen's Bastion, in András Hess Square (named after Hungary's first printer, who started work in 1473), are the remains of Castle Hill's oldest church, built by Dominican friars in the 13th century. Only its tower and one wall have survived, and they were ingeniously incorporated in 1977 by Hungarian architect Béla Pintér into the remarkable **Hilton Hotel,** which successfully combines old and new forms while blending in with neighboring buildings. At the far end of the square, a historic inn once more famous than any and all Hiltons, **Vörös Sün** (The Red Hedgehog) is now a shabby drink-and-snack bar.

Four parallel streets lead to the northern end of the Castle Hill district from the area around Szentháromság tér and Hess András tér. **Országház utca** (Parliament Street.), which extends northward from the western end of Szentháromság tér, was the main thoroughfare of 18th-century Buda; it takes its name from the building at No. 28, which was the seat of Parliament from 1790 to 1807. Before its appropriation for secular use, this building was the church and convent of the Order of St. Clare. Across the street at No. 17 is the Old Parliament Restaurant (Régi Országház) with medieval wine cellar.

Both Országház utca and Úri utca end at **Kapisztrán tér,** named after St. John of Capistrano, an Italian friar who, in 1456, recruited a crusading army to fight the Turks who were threatening Hungary. Capistrano joined forces with Janos Hunyadi, the most famous Hungarian general of the Middle Ages, and together they defended the fortress at Nandorfehervar (today's Belgrade). There's a statue of this honored Franciscan on the northwest corner of the square. On the south side of the square, all that remains of the Gothic 12th-century **Mária Magdolna-templom** (Church of St. Mary Magdalene) is its Tower *(torony)*, completed in 1496; the rest of the church was destroyed by air raids in World War II. Across the square, at the northwestern corner, is the casern housing the War History Institute and the **Hadtörténeti Intézet és Múzeum** (Museum of the Hungarian Army). The collection includes uniforms and military regalia, many belonging to Hungarian generals who took part in the abortive uprising against Austrian rule in 1848. Other exhibits trace the military history of Hungary from the original Magyar conquest in the 9th century, through the period of Ottoman rule, down to the middle of this century. *Tóth Árpád sétány 40, tel. 361/156–9522 or 361/156–9770. Admission: 15 Ft. Open Tues.–Sat. 9–5, Sun. 10–6.*

Fortuna utca, the smallest and most charming of the four streets, takes its name from an 18th-century Fortuna Inn that welcomed guests at No. 4. The inn now houses the **Kereskedelmi és Vendéglátóipari Múzeum** (Museum of Commerce and Catering). The Catering Museum contains an authentic pastry shop with genuine turn-of-the-century fixtures. *Fortuna utca 4. Admission: 20 Ft. adults, 10 Ft. children; free Fri.*

Though the houses on Fortuna utca have Baroque facades, many have Gothic windows, and their courtyards comprise any number of styles, reliefs, and carved decorations. No. 6 pays homage to Fortuna, the Roman goddess of fortune, in an early 19th-century relief. At No. 9 is a 20th-century rendition of her by the modern sculptor Ferenc Medgyessy.

Táncsics Mihály utca, the last of these four streets, loops to the north off of Hess András tér. It is named after a rebel writer imprisoned in the dungeons below the Baroque house (formerly the Royal Mint) at No. 9 and freed by the people on the Day of Revolution, March 15, 1848. The leader of that revolution, Lajos Kossuth, had also been imprisoned here from 1837 to 1840. Next door, No. 7, where Beethoven stayed in 1800 when he came to Buda to conduct his works, is the **Zenetörténeti Múzeum** (Museum of Music History) displaying rare manuscripts, instruments, and Béla Bartok's studio. *Táncsics Mihály utca 7, tel. 361/175–9011 ext. 272. Admission: 15 Ft. adults, 5 Ft. children. Open Mon. 4–9, Wed.–Sun. 10–6.*

At Táncsics Mihály utca 26 is a newly excavated two-room **Medieval Synagogue** now used as a museum. On display are objects relating to the Jewish community, including religious inscriptions, frescoes, and tombstones dating to the 15th century. There are a number of Hebrew gravestones in the entranceway. *Táncsics Mihály utca 26. Admission: 15 Ft. Open May–Oct., Tues.–Fri. 10–2, Sat., Sun., holidays 10–6.*

Fortuna utca and Táncsics Mihály utca empty into **Bécsi kapu tér** (Vienna Gate Square), which has some fine Baroque and Rococo houses. It is dominated, however, by the enormous neo-Romanesque (1913–17) headquarters of the **Hungarian National Archives** (Országos Levéltár), which looks more like a cathedral, as befits a shrine to paperwork. The gate itself, opening toward Vienna—or, closer at hand, Moszkva tér—was rebuilt in 1936.

There are many ways to descend from Castle Hill to the banks of the Danube; the easiest route leads south to the old quarter called the **Tabán** (from the Turkish word for "tanner"). A one-time suburb of Buda, it was known at the end of the 17th century as Little Serbia (*Rác*) because so many Serbian refugees settled here after fleeing from the Turks. It later became a quaint and romantic district of vineyards and small taverns. Though most of the small houses characteristic of this district have been demolished—mainly in the interests of easing auto traffic—a few picturesque buildings remain.

At Apród utca 1 is the house where Ignác Semmelweis, the great Hungarian physician and discoverer of the cause of puerperal (childbed) fever, was born in 1818. Despite the great importance of his work, Semmelweis was hounded out of Vienna in 1851 for insisting that obstetric assistants scrub their hands thoroughly to reduce the mortality rate from infection in childbirth. This rejection by his colleagues is believed to have contributed to his later decline into insanity. His splendid Baroque house is now the **Semmelweis Orvostörténeti Múzeum** (Museum of Medical History); exhibits trace the history of healing and include a number of articles and documents associated with his life. (The Hungarian prime minister, Jozsef Antal, was curator of this museum for several years before his election to parliament after the Communists surrendered power.) *Apród utca 1–3, tel. 361/175–3533. Admission: 15 Ft. Open Tues.–Sun. 10:30–5:30.*

Around the corner, at No. 1 Szarvas tér, is the **Szarvas-haz** (Stag House). This building in Louis XVI style was named after the former Szarvas café, or, more accurately, after its extant trade sign with an emblem of a stag not quite at bay, which can be seen above the triangular arched entryway. Today the structure houses the Arany Szarvas (Golden Stag) restaurant, which is renowned for its excellent game dishes and which preserves some of the mood of the old Tabán.

Walk a few yards down Szarvas tér toward the Elizabeth Bridge to reach the **Tabán plébánia-templom** (Tabán Parish Church), built in 1736 on the site of a Turkish mosque and subsequently renovated and reconstructed several times. Its present form could be described as restrained Baroque.

Walk down Attila utca to Hegyalja út and go under the end of the Erzsébet bridge to the other side of Hegyalja. You are now at the foot of the most beautiful natural formation on the Buda bank. **Gellért-hegy** (Gellért Hill), 232 meters (761 ft.) high, takes its name from Saint Gellért (Gerard) of Csanad, a Venetian bishop who came to Hungary in the 11th century and was supposedly flung to his death from the top of the hill by pagans. More misery awaits you as you ascend, but take solace from the cluster of hot springs at the foot of the hill. On the riverbank are the **Rudas Baths**, fed by eight springs with a year-round temperature of 44C (111F). Primitive baths were first built over these hot springs in the Middle Ages, and they were renewed and expanded by the Turkish pasha Mustafa Sokoli in 1566, again in the 19th century, and in 1951–52. The finest part of the building is its original Turkish pool. *Döbrentei tér 9, tel. 361/156–1322.*

Near the ramp coming off the Elizabeth Bridge is another public bath, the **Rác Baths,** built during the reign of King

Zsigmond in the early 15th century and rebuilt by Míklos Ybl in the mid-19th century (*see* Sports and Fitness, *below*).

At the southern end of the park, at the foot of the Gellert Hill just past the **Szabadsághíd** (Liberty Bridge)— are the beautiful Art Nouveau **Gellért Hotel and Thermal Baths** (*see* Lodging, *below*); visiting this complex at this point in the tour would involve a detour, unless you want to take public transport up the hill, in which case you can take trams and buses a couple of stops beyond the Gellért Hotel to Móricz Zsigmond körtér and there board bus no. 27 to the summit. If you have a car, the most direct way up to the top of the hill is via Hegyalja út (the road off the Elizabeth Bridge); turn left at the Citadella turnoff. On foot it's an easy 30-minute climb from Hegyalja út through pleasant parkland perfect for picnicking and sunbathing.

⑥ The **Citadella** fortress atop the hill was a much hated sight for Hungarians. They called it the Gellért Bastille, for it was erected on the site of an earlier wooden observatory by the Austrian army as a lookout after the 1848–49 War of Independence. Renovation as a tourist site in the 1960s improved its image with the addition of cafés, a beer garden, wine cellars, and a tourist hostel. In its inner wall is a small graphic exhibition (with some relics) of Budapest's 2,000-year history. *Admission free. Open 24 hours.*

Firework displays on August 20 (St. Stephen's and Constitution Day) became a Citadella ritual, too. Less help came from the 40-meter (130-feet) high 1947 **Liberation Memorial,** which starts just below the southern edge of the fort and towers above it. Visible from many parts of the city, it honors the 1944–45 siege of Budapest and the Russian soldiers who fell in the battle. It was the work of a noted Hungarian sculptor, Zsigmond Kisfaludi-Stróbl, and from the distance it looks light, airy, and even liberating: A sturdy young girl, her hair and robe swirling in the wind, holds a palm branch high above her head. Up close, however, her Stalin Gothic trappings weigh her down. Flanked by Red Army combat infantrymen, she is embellished with a gold hammer and sickle, sculptures of giants slaying dragons, and reliefs of workers and peasants rejoicing at the freedom that Soviet liberation failed to bring to Hungary. But the views of Budapest from the ramparts are well worth the trip.

Back down at Danube level, a northbound exploration of Buda could continue with the help of bus no. 86, which covers the waterfront, or on foot, though distances are fairly great. North of Clark Ádam tér and the Széchenyi lánchíd (Chain Bridge), in the narrow strip between Castle Hill and the Danube, some of the ambience of old Buda is preserved, but unfortunately many of the houses have been demolished. A broad promenade adorns the river embankment, and on the other side of heavy traffic cross streets climb Castle Hill. Some of them have flights of steps reminiscent of Montmartre.

⑦ **Fő utca** (Main Street), a long, straight thoroughfare, starts at the Chain Bridge and is lined with late-18th-century houses boasting impressive wrought-iron balconies. The first church you will encounter, the **Capuchin Church,** was converted from a Turkish mosque at the end of the 17th century. Damaged during the revolution in 1849, it acquired its current Romantic-style exterior when it was rebuilt a few years later. Fő utca is

⑧ punctuated by **Corvin tér,** with the turn-of-the-century **Folk**

Art Institute and Buda Concert Hall at No. 8 (tel. 361/1354–
354); by Szilágyi Dezső tér (Béla Bartok's house is at No. 4), and
again by Batthyány tér, a lovely square open on its river side to
afford a grand view of Parliament directly across the Danube.
The M2 subway, the HEV electric railway from Szentendre,
and various suburban and local buses converge on the square,
which also has a busy marketplace. At Batthyány tér 4 is the
former White Cross Inn, a Rococo mansion where gala balls
were held. It became a concert hall where Franz Liszt often
played. At No. 7 is the beautiful Baroque twin-towered Szent
Anna-templom (Church of St. Anne, 1740–62), its interior in-
spired by Italian art and its oval cupola adorned with frescoes
and statuary.

At Fő utca 84 is the royal gem of Turkish baths in Budapest, the
16th-century Király-fürdő (King Baths), its cupola crowned by
a golden moon and crescent. Diagonally across from the baths
is the Greek Szent Flórián-kapolna (Florian Chapel), built in
Rococo style between 1756 and 1760. It used to stand at the
18th-century elevation of old Buda but was recently raised to
the present street level. Fő utca ends Bem Jozsef tér, where
you'll see a statue of the Polish general Jozsef Bem, who offered
his services to the 1848 revolutionaries in Vienna and then
Hungary. Reorganizing the rebel forces in Transylvania, he in-
flicted numerous defeats on the Habsburgs and was the war's
most successful general. It was at this statue on October 23,
1956, that a great student demonstration in sympathy with
Poles striving for liberal reforms exploded into the brave and
tragic Hungarian uprising suppressed by the Red Army.

After Bem József tér (Joseph Bem Square), turn left on Feke-
tesas utca, cross the busy Mártírok útja, and turn right on
Mecset (Mosque) utca, a romantic little cobblestone street with
an Old World atmosphere that climbs up Rózsadomb (Rose Hill)
to the Tomb of Gül Baba, a 16th-century dervish and poet
whose name means "father of roses" in Turkish. He fought in
several wars waged by the Turks and fell during the siege of
Buda in 1541. His tomb, built of carved stone blocks with four
oval windows, remains a place of pilgrimages, for it is considered Europe's northernmost Moslem holy place and marks the
spot where he was slain. An Islamic Center, to be built on this
spot, will eventually incorporate the tomb. Nearby is a good
lookout location for views of Buda and across the river to Pest.
*Mecset utca 14. Admission: 20 Ft. adults, 10 Ft. children.
Open 10–6. Closed Mon. and Nov.–Apr.*

Tour 2: Margaret Island and the Danube Bridges

This tour is not to be taken as a single stroll; rather, it serves as
an orientation to several unique aspects of the Budapest landscape. True, an hourlong walk along Margaret Island between
the Árpád and Margaret bridges is self-contained; the other
bridges, however, are best examined or explored whenever
your travels take you on or near them.

Budapest has always been as proud of its bridges as Prague or
Paris, and their total destruction by the retreating Nazi armies
was as devastating as the wanton blowing-up of the Arno
bridges in Florence. For many months, only a pontoon bridge
connected Buda and Pest; but all seven bridges were eventually

rebuilt over the next two decades, and an eighth, the Árpád Bridge, was newly constructed.

Farthest north is the **Northern Railway Bridge,** reopened in 1955. It also has a walkway. The **Árpád Bridge,** opened in 1950, is the longest at 2 kilometers (1¼ miles) and widest of the eight. It connects two northern industrial suburbs, Óbuda and Újpest, and offers the only means of access by car to **Margit-sziget** (Margaret Island). Budapest's special park in the middle of the Danube, 2½ kilometers (1½ miles) long and covering nearly 80 hectares (200 acres), Margaret Island is ideal for strolling, jogging, or just delighting in the fragrances of its lawns and gardens.

The island was first mentioned almost 2,000 years ago as the summer residence of the commander of the Roman garrison at nearby Aquincum. Later known as Rabbit Island (Insula Leporum), it was a royal hunting ground during the Árpád dynasty. King Imre, who reigned from 1196 to 1204, held court here, and several convents and monasteries were built during the Middle Ages. It takes its current name from St. Margaret, the pious daughter of King Béla IV. At the age of ten, she retired to a Dominican nunnery here, where she died in 1271, at the age of 29. (She was canonized seven centuries later.) In the 19th century, the Habsburgs turned it into a landscape garden, and by the turn of this century its thermal waters had made it a spa favored by royalty, writers, and artists. From 1869 to 1928, a horse-drawn tramway criss-crossed the island.

Descending from the Árpád Bridge at the northern end of the island, you encounter a copy of the water-powered Marosvásárhely Musical Fountain, which plays songs and chimes. The original was designed more than a century-and-a-half ago by a Transylvanian named Péter Bodor. It stands near an artificial Rock Garden with Japanese dwarf trees and lily ponds. The stream coursing through it never freezes, for it comes from a natural hot spring whose healing properties have given rise to the Ramada Grand and Thermal hotels at this end of the island (*see* Lodging, *below*). Two new spa hotels facing Margaret Island, the Aquincum on the Buda bank and the Hélia on the Pest side, have their waters piped in from springs on the island.

Past the hotels, on the bank facing Pest, is the weather-beaten Premonstratensian Chapel, built in the 11th or 12th century. Its 15th-century bell, the oldest in Hungary, was found in 1949 among the roots of a walnut tree. Near it are the ruins of St. Margaret's Convent and those of the Dominican nunnery's church and burial grounds, including the empty white marble sepulcher of St. Margaret herself. They were found during excavations in 1958. Behind them is the Water Tower (1912), an early masterwork of Hungarian reinforced-concrete architecture. Next to it is an open-air theater built in 1938 as a setting for summer opera, ballet, and folklore programs. Through the center of the island runs the Artists' Promenade lined with busts of Hungarian artists, writers, and musicians. It leads past the Palatinus Baths (toward the Buda side), built in 1921, which can attract tens of thousands of people on a summer day. Nearby are a tennis stadium, a youth athletic center, boathouses, sports grounds, and, most impressive of all, the National Sports Swimming Pool (Nemzeti Sportuszoda) designed by the architect Alfred Hájos. While still in his teens, Hájos had won two gold medals in swimming at the first modern

Olympic Games, held in Athens in 1896. A Rose Garden with several thousand kinds of flowers, the Casino Restaurant (dating back to 1920), a Fountain with illuminated waters that change color at night, and a Unification monument, honoring the merger of Buda, Pest, and Óbuda in 1873, mark the approach to the Margaret Bridge at the south end of the island. Bus no. 26, traveling across the Margaret Bridge to and from the Pest side, is allowed onto and across the island.

Time Out   Beside the Rose Garden, stop for coffee at the **Kuba Espresso** in a pavilion of bamboo and handwoven raffia, in the style of a Cuban seashore café.

---

⑯ Toward the end of 1944, the **Margithíd** (Margaret Bridge) was blown up by the retreating Nazis while it was crowded with rush-hour traffic. It was rebuilt in its same unusual shape—forming an obtuse angle in midstream, with a short leg leading down to the island. The original bridge was built in the 1840s by French engineer Ernest Gouin in collaboration with Gustave Eiffel, who spent time in Hungary during the construction of the Margaret Bridge.

⑰ The oldest of the Danube Bridges is the **Lánchíd** (Chain Bridge), also known as Széchenyi-lanchid. It was built at the initiative of the great Hungarian reformer and philanthropist, Count István Széchenyi, from an 1839 design by the English civil engineer William Tierney Clark, who had also designed London's Hammersmith Bridge. This almost poetically graceful and symmetrical suspension bridge was finished ten years later by his Scottish namesake, Adam Clark. No sooner was the bridge completed than the Austrian army, during the Hungarian War of Independence, tried twice to blow it up. The first time, the Austrians filled the bridge's chambers with gunpowder, but Clark flooded the powder before it could be detonated. The second attempt saw an Austrian colonel take matters into his own hands by placing barrels of gunpowder on the roadway. He succeeded only in blowing himself up. Clark, who married a Hungarian girl and spent the rest of his life in Budapest, also built the 350-meter (383-yard) tunnel under Castle Hill, thus connecting the Danube quay with the rest of Buda. The space between bridge and tunnel has been named Adam Clark Square. On the Pest side, the Chain Bridge leads into Roosevelt tér and the heart of downtown. Before the bridge was built, the river could be crossed only by ferry or by a pontoon bridge that had to be removed when ice blocks began flowing downstream in winter. The Clarks' creation, 370 meters (405 yards) long and in Classical style, rests on twin pillars in the riverbed, each with a superstructure taking the form of a triumphal arch. After its destruction by the Nazis, the bridge was rebuilt in its original form (though slightly widened for traffic) and was reopened in 1949, on the centenary of its inauguration.

⑱ South of the Chain Bridge, the **Erzsébethíd** (Elizabeth Bridge) links several of Buda's hills with one of Pest's principal shopping streets, Kossuth Lajos utca. Built between 1897 and 1903, it was the longest single-span suspension bridge in Europe at the time. Near its western end is a seated **Statue of Empress Elizabeth,** the wife of Franz Joseph, a beautiful but unhappy anorexic who was stabbed to death in 1898 by an anarchist while boarding a boat on Lake Geneva. The Hungarians, who were particularly fond of her, named the new bridge in her memory. When the Nazis destroyed her bridge, they also damaged her statue badly. Rebuilt as a more modern and wider cable bridge, spanning the Danube in a single arch with no pier in the riverbed, the Elizabeth Bridge was the last to reopen, in 1964. It took even longer for her statue to be restored, but it was recently resurrected on a new site, where the unfortunate empress now sits closer to the bridge bearing her name.

⑲ **Szabadsághíd** (Liberty Bridge), Budapest's narrowest, is painted a distinctive green. Built between 1894 and 1896 of wrought open-hearth iron, it was originally named after Franz Joseph and was later known as Customhouse Square Bridge. It connects Gellért Hill in Buda with the museum and market quarters of Pest. As spartan and functional as Franz Joseph himself, it achieved notoriety during the 1930s depression, when many unemployed people climbed its four slender towers and leaped off the handsome eagles atop them.

⑳ The **Petőfi Bridge,** named after the great poet of the Hungarian revolution, Sandor Petőfi, is 372 meters (407 yards) long and links Buda with Pest's Outer Ring Road. Last is the 393-meter (430 yard) **Southern Railway Bridge.**

Tour 3: Pest

Downtown Pest Start with the most visible, though not highly accessible, sym-
㉑ bol of Budapest's left bank, the huge neo-Gothic **Országház** (houses of Parliament). Mirrored in the Danube much the way Britain's Parliament is reflected by the Thames, it lies midway between the Margaret and Chain bridges and is reached by the M2 subway (Kossuth tér station) and waterfront tram no. 2, though it is also within walking distance of many downtown hotels. A fine example of fin-de-siècle, historicizing, eclectic architecture, it was designed by the Hungarian architect Ímre Steindl and built by a thousand workers between 1885 and 1902. Both its exterior and interior reflect the taste of its time—grandiose yet delicate. "I used the flowers of Hungary's fields, meadows, and forests in a stylized form," the architect explained. The grace and dignity of its long facade and 24 slender towers, with spacious arcades and high windows balancing its vast central dome, lend this living landmark a refreshingly Baroque spatial effect. The outside is lined with 90 statues of great figures in Hungarian history; the corbels are ornamented by 242 allegorical statues. Inside are 691 rooms, ten courtyards, and 29 staircases; some 40 kilos (88 pounds) of gold were used for the staircases and halls. These halls are also a gallery of late-19th-century Hungarian art with frescoes and canvases depicting Hungarian history, starting with Mihály Munkácsy's large painting of the Magyar Conquest of 896. With its ornamental staircase, star-studded vault, and pillars crowned with kings of Hungary and princes of Transylvania, the hall beneath the cupola is an explosion of glitter like a display of fireworks. The **Parliament Library** has Kossuth's handwritten journals. Unfortunately, because Parliament is a workplace for legislators, the building is not open to individual visitors and must be toured in groups at certain hours on specific city tours organized by IBUSZ (tel. 361/1185-707), Budapest Tourist (tel. 361/1173-555), and Omnibusz Travel (tel. 361/1172-511).

Dominated by the Parliament building, this district is the legislative, diplomatic, and administrative nexus of Budapest; most of the ministries are here, as are the National Bank and Courts of Justice. One of the buildings, an 1890s neo-Classical temple opposite Parliament formerly housed the Supreme Court and is proclaimed by such allegorical statuary as *Lawmaker and Master of Laws, Condemned and Acquitted, Public Prosecutor and Defender*. It is now the **Néprajzi Múzeum** (Museum of Ethnography), tracing the evolution of societies from prehistoric to modern times. There are special collections of Hungarian folk art and folklore as well as the art of Oceania. *Kossuth tér 12, tel. 361/132-6340. Admission: 20 Ft. adults, 10 Ft. children. Open Tues.-Sun. 10-6. Occasional guided tours in English. Choral concerts Sun. 11 AM Oct.-July.*

In Kossuth Square are statues not only of Kossuth but also of Rákóczi as well as Mihály Károlyi, president of the short-lived Hungarian republic at the end of World War I, and the poet Attila József. Vecsey ut, slanting side street at the southeast corner of Kossuth tér, leads to **Szabadságtér (Liberty Square)**, where another solemn-looking neo-Classical shrine, the **National Bank,** mixes Baroque and Art Nouveau inside. It is dwarfed, however, by the neighboring **Hungarian Television Headquarters,** a former stock exchange of Disneyland proportions, with what look like four temples and two castles on its roof.

Szabadság tér was just a pleasant detour, so rejoin Nádor utca—which leads south from Kossuth tér toward the heart of downtown—passing, at No. 23, Franz Liszt's first apartment in Budapest. At Vigyázó utca, turn right, toward the river, and enter **Roosevelt tér.** It is less closely connected with any U.S. President than with the progressive Hungarian statesman, Count István Széchenyi, whom even his adversary, Kossuth, dubbed "the greatest Hungarian." The neo-Renaissance palace of the **Academy of Sciences** on your right was built between 1862 and 1864, after Széchenyi's suicide. It is a fitting memorial, for it was he who, back in 1825, had donated a year's income from all his estates to establish the Academy. Another Széchenyi project, the Chain Bridge (Széchenyi-lánchíd: *see* Tour 2), leads into the square, in which a statue of Széchenyi stands near one of another statesman, Ferenc Deák, whose negotiations led to the establishment of the dual monarchy after Kossuth's 1848-49 revolution failed. Both men lived on this square.

Facing the Danube at Roosevelt tér 5-6 is a shabby but astonishing Art Nouveau wonder, the **Gresham Building,** completed in 1906 for a British life insurance company. Lilies and peacocks adorn its iron gateway. The main modern attraction of this rundown monumental block, a Chinese restaurant, recently gave way to a gambling casino, which may find it advantageous to upgrade its cultural image by restoring the building's past glitter and glory.

The neighborhood to its south has, after all, regained much of its past elegance—if not its architectural grandeur—with the erection of the Atrium Hyatt, Forum, and Duna Inter-Continental luxury hotels. Traversing all three and continuing well beyond them is the riverside **Korzó,** a pedestrian promenade lined with appealing outdoor cafés and restaurants.

Time Out   The most inviting sidewalk café along the Korzó, **DuBarry,** is also called the **Ambassador** or, by its owners' name, **Schuk & Schuk.** Desserts and a small menu of hot main dishes, half of which are already "out" by noon, change from day to day but are invariably first-rate; should you smell stuffed cabbage, search no further for your selection. Service is offhand but friendly—unless you want something difficult, like the house's street address or calling card, in which case you will be avoided like the plague. Phone 1188–572 if you want to be told how to get there, but suffice it to say that this quirky oasis lies between the Forum Hotel (whose Viennese Coffeehouse serves the best cream pastries in town) and the Duna-Corsó Restaurant (*see* Dining, *below*) next door.

㉖ After passing Duna-Corsó's outdoor tables, turn left into **Vigadó tér,** which takes its name from the **Vigadó Concert Hall** at No. 2. Designed in a striking Romantic style by Frigyes Feszl and inaugurated in 1865 with Franz Liszt conducting his own *St. Elizabeth Oratorio*, it is a curious mixture of Byzantine, Moorish, Romanesque, and Hungarian motifs. It is punctuated by dancing statues and sturdy pillars.

Brahms, Debussy, and Casals are among the other immortals who have graced its stage. Mahler's First Symphony and many works by Bartók were first performed here. Severely damaged in World War II, the Vigadó was rebuilt and reopened in 1980. Its restaurant is recommended and reasonable.

Continue along the Korzó past the bunkerlike Inter-Continental Hotel. Just before you reach a statue of the revolutionary poet Sándor Petőfi, find your way (usually through a side entrance) into the **Greek Orthodox Church** at Petőfi tér 2/b. Built at the end of the 18th century in late-Baroque style, it was remodeled a century later by Miklós Ybl who designed the Opera House and many other landmarks that give today's Budapest its monumental appearance. The church retains some fine wood-carvings and a dazzling array of icons by a late-18th-century Serbian master, Miklós Jankovich.

㉗ The Korzó ends at **Március (March) 15th tér,** bisected by the Elizabeth Bridge and flanked by two of Pest's more touristy restaurants, Mátyás Pince and Százéves. The ground is lower here, for you are walking around the remains of the **Contra Aquincum,** a third-century Roman fortress and tower. Built on its walls at Március 15th tér 2 is the oldest ecclesiastical building in Pest, **Belvárosi plébánia templom (Inner City Parish Church).** It dates back to the 12th century, and there is hardly any architectural style that cannot be found in some part or other—starting with a single Romanesque arch in its south tower. The single nave still has its original Gothic chancel and some 15th-century Gothic frescoes. Two side chapels contain beautifully carved Renaissance altarpieces and tabernacles of red marble from the early 16th century. During Budapest's years of Turkish occupation, the church served as a mosque—and this is remembered by a mihrab, a Muslim prayer niche. In the 18th century, it was baroqued with two towers and its present facade. In 1808, it was enriched with a Rococo pulpit, and still later a superb winged triptych was added to the main altar. From 1867 to 1875, Franz Liszt lived only a few steps away from the church, in a town house where he held regular "musical Sundays" at which Richard and Cosima Wagner were frequent guests and participants. Liszt's own musical Sunday mornings often began in this church. An admirer of its acoustics and organ, he conducted many masses here, including the first Budapest performance of his Missa Choralis, in 1872. In the 20th century, the church had to be slightly narrowed for the widening of the Elizabeth Bridge.

㉘ Paralleling the Korzó is Budapest's best-known shopping street, **Váci utca,** a pedestrian precinct with electrified 19th-century lampposts, smart shops with chic window displays and credit-card emblems on ornate doorways, and most of the international brand names that long ago (and, perhaps, prematurely) won Budapest the accolade of the "Paris of the East." No bargain basement, Váci utca takes its special flavor from the mix of native clothiers, furriers, tailors, dress designers, shoemakers, folk artists, and others who offer affordable alternatives to the global-boutique superstars. There are also bookstores—first- and secondhand in addition to foreign-language—and china and crystal shops, as well as gourmet food stores redolent of paprika. With rapid democratization, street commerce on Váci utca has shifted to a freer market: news vendors hawk today's Western press. Outside the city's largest folk-art shop, one runs a gauntlet of peasant women in kerchiefs and long skirts, farmers in fur hats and brightly colored jackets, and Transylvanians in full uniform all peddling hand-embroidered linens, dirndls, and ceramics. Artistically cut and woven barbed wire from the dismantled Iron Curtain is also for sale—gift wrapped.

If you are more interested in the street's architecture than in its wares, gaze up at the statuary, facades, and colors of the buildings above the storefronts. But no matter how high your eyes and soul soar, protect your wallet at pickpocket level. And don't feel obliged to explore Váci utca in tandem with the Korzó. Regardless of when you prefer to patrol shopping precincts, fit Váci utca and its interesting side streets—Régi Posta utca, with Hungary's first McDonald's, and Kígyó utca, another fashionable mall—into your schedule accordingly. In either event, whether you turn left at the Inner City Parish Church or off Váci utca near the Elizabeth Bridge, you will rejoin our tour on Kossuth Lajos utca, a popular and less pricy—but heavily trafficked and polluted—shopping street.

㉙ Cross Kossuth Lajos utca at Ferenciek tér to reach the **Franciscan Church** (1743). On the wall is a bronze relief showing a scene from the devastating flood of 1838, which swept away many houses and lives; the detail is so vivid that it could almost make you seasick (or is that the air poisoning this congested artery?). An arrow below the relief indicates the highwater mark of more than a meter (almost four feet). Next to it is the **Fountain of the Nereides,** a popular meeting place that elaborates the square's nautical motif.

㉚ Following Károlyi Mihály utca past the Franciscan Church and the Loránd Eötvös University Library to **Egyetem tér** (University Square) leads to the cool gray-and-green marble **University Church,** one of Hungary's best and most beautiful Baroque buildings. Built between 1725 and 1742, it boasts an especially splendid pulpit. Around the corner, on Szerb utca, is a **Serbian orthodox church** (1688) that is one of Budapest's oldest buildings.

Time Out Szerb utca meets the nonpedestrian continuation of Váci utca near the Serbian Church. If you follow Váci utca past the Liberty Bridge, crossing Vámház körút (Customshouse Boulevard, until recently named Tolbuhin after a World War II Soviet military commander), you will come to the waterfront's neo-Renaissance ex-Customs House. Built in 1871–74 by Miklós Ybl, it is now the **University of Economics** after a stint as Karl Marx University. In nearby Fővám tér (Customshouse Square, formerly Dimitrov), is the gigantic **Central Market Hall,** an interesting 19th-century iron-frame construction within which, even during the leanest years of communist shortages, the abundance of food came as a revelation to visitors from East and West. You may have to be content with an exterior view: the market was closed for repairs in 1991 and may not reopen for several years.

Return on Szerb utca to Egyetem ter, turning right on Kecskeméti utca and passing beneath the connecting bridge of the spanking new Hotel Korona; or else follow Vámház körút **③** from the Market Hall. Either way, you will enter **Kálvin tér** (Calvin Square), which takes its name from the neo-Classical **Protestant Church** that tries to dominate this busy traffic hub. Here once stood a main gate of Pest, the Kecskeméti Kapu, and a cattle market that was also a den of thieves. At the beginning of the 19th century, this was where Pest ended and the prairie began.

Modern Pest is laid out in broad circular boulevards (körúts), and **Vámház körút** is the first sector of the 2.7-kilometer (1.7-mile) **Inner Körút,** which traces the old town wall from the Liberty Bridge to the Nyugati (West) Railway Station. Construction of the Inner Körút began in 1872 and was completed in 1880. Changing names as it curves, after Kalvin tér it becomes Múzeum körút.

㉜ The **Magyar Nemzeti Múzeum** (Hungarian National Museum), built between 1837 and 1847, is a fine example of 19th-century classicism—simple, well proportioned, and surrounded by a large garden. Before this building on March 15, 1848, Sándor Petofi recited his revolutionary poem, the National Song (Nemzeti dal), and the 12 Points, a list of political demands by young Hungarians and calling upon the people to rise against the Habsburgs.

The museum's most sacred treasure, the **Holy Crown,** reposes with other royal relics in a domed Hall of Honor off the main lobby. The crown sits like a golden soufflé above a Byzantine band of holy scenes in enamel and pearl and other gems. It seems to date from the 12th century, so it could not be the crown that Pope Sylvester II presented to St. Stephen in the year 1000, when he was crowned the first king of Hungary. Nevertheless, it is known as the Crown of St. Stephen and along with the scepter, orb (golden ball), sword, and exquisitely delicate coronation mantle also on display has long been regarded—even by communist governments—as the legal symbol of Hungarian sovereignty and unbroken statehood for nearly a millennium. In 1945 the fleeing Hungarian army handed over the crown and its accompanying regalia to the Americans, rather than have them fall into Soviet hands. In 1978 they were restored to Hungary.

Atop an ornamental grand staircase flanked by frescoes are
two permanent exhibitions. "The Prehistory of the Hungarian
People from the Paleolithic Age to the Magyar Conquest" (of
896) displays Stone, Bronze, and Iron Age relics and a collection of princely treasures from the Great Migrations. "The History of the Hungarian People from the Magyar Conquest to
1848" starts with a display of jewels, attire, and armor of the
Magyar tribes and continues with a comprehensive presentation of Christianization and subsequent Hungarian development. Exhibit captions and periodic narratives posted on
walls are translated into English. Among the rarities in this often surprising treasure trove are an early 15th-century saddle
adorned with small bone plates and showing knights and horses
and scenes of chivalry. It was made in a Buda workshop for the
15th-century King Sigismund of Luxembourg, later Holy Roman Emperor. There is also a completely furnished Turkish
tent; masterworks of cabinetmaking and wood carving, including pews from churches in Nyírbátor and Transylvania; a piano
that belonged to both Beethoven and Liszt; and, in the treasury, masterpieces of goldsmithery, among them the 11th-cen-
tury Constantions Monomachos crown from Byzantium and the
richly pictorial 16th-century chalice of Miklós Pálffy. Looking
at it is like reading the "Prince Valiant" comic strip in gold.
*Múzeum körút 14–16, tel. 361/1382–122. Admission: 30 Ft.
adults, 15 Ft. children. Open Tues.–Sun. 10–6.*

Continue along Múzeum körút past the major intersection—
Astoria, once the Hatvani Gate in the 15th-century city wall—
where it becomes Tanács körút. At Dohány utca stands the
㉝ **Great Synagogue,** Europe's largest, designed by Ludwig Förs-
ter and built between 1844 and 1859 in a Byzantine-Moorish
style described as "consciously archaic Romantic-Eastern."
Desecrated by German and Hungarian Nazis, it is being reconstructed with donations from all over the world with particular
help from the Emanuel Foundation, named after actor Tony
Curtis's father, the late Emanuel Schwartz, who emigrated
from Budapest to the Bronx. In the courtyard, a weeping willow made of metal honors the victims of the Holocaust. Liszt
and Saint-Saens are among the great musicians who have
played its grand organ. *Dohány utca 2–8. Admission free.
Open Mon.–Fri. 10–1 except when there are ceremonies.*

Around the corner is the **National Jewish Museum,** with relics
from the history of Hungarian Jewry. *Dohány utca 2, tel. 361/
1428–949. Admission: 20 Ft. adults, 10 Ft. children. Open
May–Oct., Tues.–Fri. and Sun. 10–1; Mon. and Thurs. 2–6.*

Tanács körút (Council Boulevard) owes its name to the monumental City Council building, which used to be a hospital for
wounded soldiers and then an old-age resort ("home" would be
㉞ too cozy for so vast a hulk). It is now **Városház** (City Hall), overlooking the boulevard but entered through courtyards or side
streets (Gerlóczy utca is the most accessible). Its 57-window facade, interrupted by five projections, fronts on Városház utca,
which parallels the körút. The Tuscan columns at the main entrance and the allegorical statuary of Atlas, War, and Peace,
are especially splendid. There was once a chapel in the center of
the main facade, but now only its spire remains. The project
was begun in 1716 under the direction of an Italian and a Viennese architect, Fortunato da Prati and Johann Holbling, and 10
masons. It was completed by Anton Erhard Martinelli between

1727 and 1735. In the colorful adjoining square named after him, Martinelli tér, is the **Church of the Servite Order,** built in Martinelli's last years, but its facade was redone in 1871 with columns and a statue of the Virgin Mary.

At **Deák tér,** where all three subway lines converge, is the neo-Classical **Lutheran Church,** built by Mihály Pollack starting in 1799, nearly 40 years before the National Museum was built from his design. The Lutheran Church's interior designer, János Krausz, flouted traditional church architecture of the time by placing a single large interior beneath the huge vaulted roof structure. The adjoining school, which the revolutionary poet Petőfi attended in 1833–34, is now the **Evangélikus Múzeum** (Lutheran Museum), tracing the role of Protestantism in Hungarian history. *Deák Ferenc tér 4, tel. 361/1174–173. Admission: 10 Ft. adults, 5 Ft. children. Open Tues.–Sun. 10–6.*

Funneling briefly off Deák tér toward Váci utca is Budapest's shortest street, **Sütő utca,** but its handful of addresses contains a key one for visitors. **Tourinform,** the Hungarian National Tourist Information Office at No. 2 (tel. 361/1179–800), is open every day of the year from 8 to 8 and is staffed by the most helpful multilingual people in Hungary. They can give you good advice and maps; book lodgings, sightseeing tours, or out-of-town trips; sell you theater tickets and guidebooks; or just listen to your problems and help you to cope.

Deák tér overlaps **Erzsébet tér** (Elizabeth Square), which was Engels tér until 1990 and, in the previous century, New Market Square—with 8,000 stands, one of Europe's largest. It is now more of a passenger marketplace, with Budapest's main bus terminal for international and long-distance buses as well as airport service.

Here the Kis (Inner) Körút becomes Bajcsy-Zsilinszky út, which we leave just past its intersection with Andrássy út and József Attila utca, turning left into Szent István tér to face the very Holy Roman front porch—its tympanum bustling with statuary—of the **Szent István Bazilika** (St. Stephen's Basilica). The city's largest church, it can hold 8,500 people. Second only to Parliament's, which is closer to the river, its dome is the most visible in the Pest skyline. This is no accident, for, with the Magyar Millennium of 1896 in mind, both domes were consciously planned to be 96 meters (315 feet) high. While Parliament's dome fell almost a meter (a yard) short, St. Stephen's was right on target. The two great spires that flank the basilica's cupola lend an added distinctiveness.

The millennium was not yet in sight when architect József Hild began building the basilica in neo-Classical style in 1851, two years after the revolution was suppressed. After Hild's death in 1867, however, the project was taken over by Miklós Ybl, the architect who did the most to transform modern Pest into a monumental metropolis—in contrast to medieval Buda across the river. Wherever he could, Ybl shifted Hild's motifs toward the neo-Renaissance mode that he favored. When the dome collapsed, partly damaging the walls, he made even more drastic changes with the millennium approaching. Ybl died in 1891, five years before the thousand-year celebration, and the basilica was completed in neo-Renaissance style by József Kauser—but not until 1905.

Below the cupola, the interior is surprisingly cool and restful, a rich collection of late-19th-century Hungarian art: mosaics, altarpieces, and statuary (what heady days the millennium must have meant for local talents!). There are 150 kinds of marble, all from Hungary except for the Carrara in the sanctuary's centerpiece: a white statue of King (St.) Stephen I, Hungary's first king and patron saint. Stephen's mummified right hand is preserved here as a relic and put on display each year on August 20, the saint's name day. *Open Mon.-Sat. 9-5 and Sun. 1-5 and for services, which are for worshipers only.*

Andrássy ut   Behind the basilica, back at the crossroad along Bajcsy-Zsilinszky út, begins Budapest's grandest avenue, **Andrássy út.** For too many years, this broad boulevard of music and mansions bore the tongue-twisting, mind-bending name of Népköztársaság (Avenue of the People's Republic) and, for a while before then, Stalin Avenue. In 1990, however, it reverted to its old name honoring Count Gyula Andrássy, a statesman who in 1867 became the first constitutional premier of Hungary. The boulevard that would eventually bear his name was begun in 1872, as Buda and Pest (and Óbuda) were about to be unified. Most of the mansions that line it were completed by 1884. It took another dozen years before the first **Underground Railway** on the Continent was completed for—you guessed it!—the Magyar Millennium in 1896. Though preceded by London's underground (1863), Budapest's was the world's first electrified subway. Only slightly modernized, this "Little Metro" (as it became known in the "Paris of Middle Europe") is still running a 3.7-kilometer (2.3-mile) stretch from Vörösmarty Square to the far end of the City Park. Using tiny yellow trains with tanklike treads, and stopping at antique stations marked "FÖLDALATTI" (underground) on their wrought-iron entranceways, Line 1 is a tourist attraction in itself. (Lines 2 and 3 weren't built until 90 years later.) Six of its 10 stations are along Andrássy út.

For this tour, however, you are urged first to walk the 2-kilometer (1¼-mile) length of Andrássy út from downtown to Heroes' Square and, after exploring the City Park beyond it, to take the Földalatti back to town. The first third of the avenue, from Bajcsy-Zsilinszky út to the Octogon crossing, boasts a row of eclectic city palaces with balconies held up by stone giants. The best of them happens to be visitable, for in an apartment with frescoes by Károly Lotz (whose work adorned the basilica and the National Museum's grand staircase) and a fine marble fireplace, is the **Postamúzeum** (Postal Museum), with an exhibition on the history of Hungarian mail, radio, and telecommunications. *Andrássy út 3, tel. 361/142793. Admission: 20 Ft. Open 10-6. Closed Mon.*

At Andrássy út 22 stands Miklós Ybl's crowning achievement, the **Opera House,** built between 1875 and 1884 in neo-Renaissance style. There are those who prefer its architecture to that of the Vienna State Opera, which it resembles on a smaller scale, and to the Paris Opera, which could swallow it up whole. Badly damaged during the siege of 1944-45, Budapest's Opera was restored to its original splendor for its 1984 centenary. Two marble sphinxes guard the driveway; the main entrance is flanked by Alajos Stróbl's "Romantic-Realist" limestone statues of Liszt and of another 19th-century Hungarian composer, Ferenc Erkel, the father of Hungarian opera. (His patriotic

Bánk bán is still performed for national celebrations.) On the facade are smaller statues of composers and muses.

Inside, the spectacle begins even before the performance. You glide up grand staircases and through wood-paneled corridors and gilded lime-green salons into a glittering jewel box of an auditorium. Its four tiers of boxes are held up by helmeted sphinxes beneath a frescoed ceiling that is also the work of Lotz. Lower down, there are frescoes everywhere, with intertwined motifs of Apollo and Dionysus. In its early years, the Budapest Opera was conducted by Gustav Mahler (from 1888 to 1891) and, after World War II, by Otto Klemperer. The acoustics are good, the stage is deep, and the excellent orchestra is elegant in white tie and tails. The singing can vary from awful to great, and tickets are relatively cheap and easy to come by, at least by tourist standards. And descending from La Bohème into the Földalatti (underground) station beneath the opera house has been described by travel writer Stephen Brook in *The Double Eagle* (1988) as stepping "out of one period piece and into another."

Across the street from the Opera House is the French Renaissance-style Drechsler Palace at Andrássy út 25. An early work by Ödön Lechner, Hungary's master of Art Nouveau, it is now the home of the National Ballet School. Behind it, a playful Art Nouveau building at Paulay Ede utca 35 houses the Children's Theatre. This is Budapest's Broadway: one block past the Opera, Nagymező utca contains three theaters, a political cabaret, a cinema, and the Moulin Rouge nightclub.

39 The culture trail continues at the next corner, Liszt Ferenc tér; at No. 8, two blocks to the right off Andrássy út, is the **Franz Liszt Academy of Music,** which, along with the Vigado, visited earlier, is the city's main concert hall. Actually, the academy has two auditoriums: a green- and gold-ornamented 1,200-seat main hall and a smaller hall for chamber music and solo concerts. Outside this exuberant Art Nouveau building, opened in 1907, Liszt reigns enthroned on the facade; the statue is by Strobl, who did him standing up outside the Opera House. The Academy has been operating as a teaching institute for almost 120 years; Liszt was its first chairman and Erkel, its first director. The pianist Ernő (formerly Ernst) Dohnányi and composers Béla Bartók and Zoltán Kodály were teachers here.

Andrássy út alters when it crosses the Outer Ring Road (Nagy körút), at the eight-sided intersection called Octogon. Four rows of trees and scores of flower beds make the thoroughfare look more like a garden promenade, but its cultural character lingers. No. 67 was the original location of the old Academy of **40** Music; entered around the corner, it now houses the **Franz Liszt Memorial Museum.** *Vörösmarty utca 3, tel. 361/1427–320. Admission: 20 Ft. Open Mon.–Fri. 10–6, Sat. 9–5. Closed Sun. Chamber concert Sept.–July, Sat. 11 AM.*

The templelike eclectic building at Andrássy 69 houses the **Puppet Theater,** and at No. 71, the **Academy of Fine Arts,** in a neo-Renaissance version of a Tuscan palace decorated with graffiti. Three blocks farther is the **Kodály Körönd,** a handsome traffic circle with imposing statues of three Hungarian warriors—leavened by a fourth one of a poet—surrounded by plane and chestnut trees. The circle takes its name from the composer Zoltán Kodály, who lived just beyond it at Andrássy út 89.

The rest of Andrássy út is dominated by widely spaced mansions surrounded by private gardens. At No. 101 is the **National Association of Hungarian Journalists**; its restaurant is open to the public daily from noon to midnight. Next door is the **Ferenc Hopp Museum of Eastern Asiatic Arts**, housing a rich collection of exotica from the Indian subcontinent and Far Eastern ceramics. *Andrássy út 103, tel. 361/1228–476. Admission: 20 Ft. adults, 10 Ft. children. Open Tues.–Sun. 10–6.*

41 Andrássy út ends in grandeur at **Hősök Tere** (Heroes' Square), with Budapest's answer to Berlin's Brandenburg Gate. The **Millennial Monument** is a semicircular twin colonnade with statues of Hungary's kings and leaders between its pillars. Set back in its open center, a 36-meter (118-foot) stone column is crowned by a dynamic statue of the Archangel Gabriel, his outstretched arms bearing the ancient emblems of Hungary. At its base ride seven bronze horsemen: the Magyar chieftains, led by Árpád, whose tribes conquered the land in 896. Most of the statues were sculpted by György Zala, whose rendition of Gabriel won him a Grand Prix in Paris in 1900. Before the column lies a simple marble slab, the **National War Memorial**, the nation's altar, at which every visiting foreign dignitary lays a ceremonial wreath. In 1991, Pope John Paul II conducted a mass here. Just a few months earlier, half a million Hungarians had convened to recall the memory of Imre Nagy, the martyred reform communist prime minister of the 1956 revolution and a nonperson for nearly 35 years.

Heroes' Square is flanked by two monumental art galleries, both built by Albert Schickedanz and Fülöp Herzog, who also collaborated on the Millennial Monument. On your right from Andrássy út is the city's largest hall for special exhibitions, the **42** **Műcsarnok** (Art Gallery), an 1895 temple of culture with a colorful tympanum. Strong on Hungarian modern art and contemporary foreign art—with frequent performances and happenings as well as a cinema—it has a loyal public of its own. *Hősök tere, tel. 361/1122–740. Admission: 20 Ft. adults, 10 Ft. children. Open Tues. 10–8, Wed.–Sun. 10–6.*

43 On your left is the **Szépművészeti Múzeum** (Museum of Fine Arts), begun in 1900 and opened in 1906. It houses Hungary's finest collection, rich in Flemish and Dutch Old Masters. With seven fine El Grecos and five beautiful Goyas as well as paintings by Velázquez and Murillo, the collection of Spanish Old Masters is considered by many to be the best outside Spain. Dutch and Flemish masters are represented by three Rembrandts as well as works by Frans Hals, Rubens, Memling, Brueghel the Elder, Van Eyck, and Van Dyck. The Italian School is represented by Giorgione, Bellini, Correggio, Tintoretto, and Titian masterpieces and, above all, two superb Raphael paintings: his *Eszterházy Madonna* and immortal *Portrait of a Youth*, rescued after a world-famous art heist. Dürer, Cranach, Altdorfer, and Hans Holbein the Elder head the German delegation; Hogarth, Reynolds, and Gainsborough, the British.

Nineteenth-century French art includes works by Delacroix, Courbet, Pissarro, Cezanne, Toulouse-Lautrec, Bonnard, Gauguin, Renoir, Utrillo, Manet, and Monet. The sculpture collection covers the 4th to 18th centuries and includes a small equestrian bronze statuette attributed to Leonardo da Vinci. There is also a display of more than 100,000 drawings (including five by Rembrandt and three studies by Leonardo), Egyptian and Greco-Roman exhibitions, late-Gothic winged altars from northern Hungary and Transylvania, and works by all the leading figures of Hungarian art up to present. *Dózsa György út 41, tel. 361/1429-759. Admission: 20 Ft. adults, 10 Ft. children. Open Apr.-Dec., Tues.-Sun. 10-6. Occasional guided tours in English.*

Városliget Heroes' Square is the gateway to the **Városliget** (City Park): a square kilometer (almost half a square mile) of recreation, entertainment, beauty, and culture calculated to delight children and adults alike. A bridge behind the Millennial Monument leads across a boating basin that becomes an artificial ice-skating rink in winter; to the south of this lake stands a **statue of George Washington,** erected in 1906 with donations by Hungarian emigrants to the United States. On an island in the lake stands **Vajdahunyad Castle,** an art historian's Disneyland named after the Transylvanian home (today in Hunedoara, Rumania) of János Hunyadi, a 15th-century Hungarian hero in the struggle against the Turks. This fantastic medley borrows from all of Hungary's historic and architectural past, starting with the Romanesque gateway of the cloister of Jak in western Hungary. A Gothic castle, Transylvanian turrets, Renaissance loggia, Baroque portico, and Byzantine decoration are all guarded by a spooky modern (1903) bronze statue of the anonymous medieval chronicler who was the first recorder of Hungarian history. Designed for the millennial celebration in 1896 but not completed until 1908, this hodgepodge houses the surprisingly interesting **Mezőgazdasági Múzeum** (Agricultural museum) with intriguingly arranged sections on animal husbandry, forestry, horticulture, hunting, and fishing. *Vajdahunyad vár, tel. 361/1423-011. Admission: 20 Ft. adults, 10 Ft. children. Open Tues.-Sat. 10-5, Sun. 10-6. Occasional guided tours in English. Folk music concerts, Sept.-June, Sun. 11 AM. Open-air brass-band concerts July-Aug., Sun. 11 AM.*

Wandering counterclockwise through the City Park, you will encounter the **Transport Museum** with its collection of old vehicles. *Városliget körút 11, tel. 361/1420-565. Admission: 20 Ft. adults, 10 Ft. children, free Wed. Open Wed.-Sun. 10-6. Videos and occasional guided tours in English. Model railway demonstrations weekdays 11 AM, Sat. and Sun. hourly.*

Petőfi Hall is a leisure-time youth center on the site of an old industrial exhibition. The vast **Széchenyi Baths** are in a fine neo-Baroque building erected between 1909 and 1913; the complex was expanded in 1926 with the addition of open-air thermal pools where you can swim outdoors even in winter. The park is also the permanent home of the **Fővárosi Nagycirkusz** (Municipal Grand Circus), which has been in business since 1878 and still gives two shows a day, year-round. Two other popular areas are the **Zoological** and **Botanical Gardens.** The latter is rich with 2,124 species of plants; the former is a fairly depressing urban zoo brightened—for humans, anyway—by an elephant pavilion decorated with Zsolnay majolica and glazed ceramic animals. Opened in 1886, the complex was designed by the Transylvanian architect and painter Károly Kós.

Because of the park's thermal waters, it was the first zoo on the Continent where a hippopotamous calved in captivity.

You have now come full circle through the City Park and back to Heroes' Square. From here, spectator-sport enthusiasts can follow Olof Palme sétány for ½ kilometer (⅓ mile) and then go one long block along Népstadion út to a sports complex dominated by the new indoor **Sportcsarnok** (Sports Hall), which can seat over 12,000 and is also used for pop concerts, ice shows, and international congresses; it is near the vast 24-hectare (60-acre) outdoor Népstadion (People's Stadium), which opened in 1953 and can hold some 96,000 people. There are also smaller arenas and a Museum of Physical Education and Sports, featuring athletic medals. *Dózsa György utca 3, tel. 361/1636–430. Admission: 20 Ft. adults, 10 Ft. children. Open Tues.–Sun. 10–6.*

Eastern Pest and the Great Ring Road If you don't plan to make the trip out to the Physical Education Museum, board the Földalatti at Heroes' Square, and ride it back to town. You can get off either at the next-to-last stop, Deák tér, or at the terminus, Vörösmarty tér. Try Deák tér if you want to visit the Subway Museum, situated in the Földalatti's 19th-century tunnel and telling the story of its construction. *Deák tér Metro station, tel. 361/1422–130. Admission: 20 Ft. adults, 10 Ft. children. Open Wed.–Sun. 10–6.*

From Deák tér, Deák utca leads to Vörösmarty tér at the northern end of the Váci utca shopping mall. Grouped around a white marble statue of the 19th-century poet and dramatist, Mihály Vörösmarty are luxury shops, airline offices, and an elegant former pissoir. Now a lovely kiosk, it displays gold-painted historic scenes of the square's golden days, which may be returning since its 1984 restoration.

Time Out The best-known, tastiest, and most tasteful address on Vörösmarty Square belongs to the **Gerbeaud** pastry shop (Vörösmarty tér 7, tel. 1181–311), founded in 1858 by a French confectioner, Henri Kugler, and later taken over by the Swiss family Gerbeaud. Filling most of a square block, it offers at least 100 kinds of sweets at any time (as well as ice cream, sandwiches, coffee, and other drinks), served in a salon setting of green marble tables and Regency-style marble fireplaces. Chocolate and cream pastries and poppy-seed croissants will never disappoint. Just visit the marble pastry counter, and point to the concoctions that interest you most. You will be given a slip of paper. Hand it to your waitress, who'll bring your choices to you.

Retrace your steps along Váci utca to Kossuth Lajos utca, but this time turn left instead of crossing Budapest's busiest shopping street. Try to look above and beyond the store windows to the architecture and activity along Kossuth Lajos utca and its continuation, Rákóczi út. As soon as you take your left onto Kossuth Lajos utca you'll see twin towers on either side of the heavily trafficked thoroughfare. They are the **Klotild** and **Matild Buildings,** built in an interesting combination of Art Nouveau and eclectic styles, which house the headquarters of the IBUSZ travel agency, the Lido Nightclub, and an advertising agency, among other tenants. At the corner of Petőfi Sándor utca, on the site of the former Inner City Savings Bank, are the **Paris Arcades,** a glass-roofed network of passages with boutiques and cafés. Built in 1914 in neo-Gothic and eclectic styles, they are among the most attractive and atmospheric meccas of downtown Pest.

Continue down Kossuth Lajos utca to the Kis (Inner) Körút at Astoria, which is where it becomes **Rákóczi út.** It is so named because it was on the 1906 route of the procession that brought back the remains of Prince Ferenc II Rákóczi of Transylvania, hero of an early 18th-century uprising against the Habsburgs, nearly two centuries after he died in defeat and exile in Turkey. At No. 21, the Moorish-style building of the **Uránia Cinema** also houses the College of Dramatic and Film Arts, which has its Studio Theater and other sections around the corner on Vas utca.

On the corner of Rákóczi út and Gyulai Pál utca stands the charming yellow 18th-century **St. Roch Chapel,** its impact rendered even more colorful by peasant women peddling lace and embroidery on its small square. The chapel is the oldest remnant of Pest's former outer district. It was built beside a hospice where doomed victims of the great plague of 1711 were sent to die as far away as possible from residential areas. The former St. Roch Hospital next door at No. 2 Gyulai Pál utca is now the **Semmelweis Hospital.** The section along Rákóczi út was built in 1841 on the site of the old hospice; the wing on Gyulai Pál utca dates to 1798. In front of the building stands a marble statue of Semmelweis. The next major intersection, **Blaha Lujza tér,** is better known to the natives as Emke and, like the Astoria crossing, is marked with a hotel bearing its name. A famous theater once stood to the right, in front of where the Corvin Department Store is now. Opposite is the headquarters of the Hírlap publishing empire.

The rest of Rákóczi út is lined with hotels, shops, and department stores, but at No. 57 is the **Lutheran Church** of the Slovak minority in Hungary. A right turn onto Luther utca leads into **Köztársaság tér** (Square of the Republic) and the city's second opera house, the **Ferenc Erkel Theatre.** Budapest's largest, with 3,000 seats, it was built in 1910–11 and offers concerts on Monday evenings. This square, where the Communist Party of Budapest had its headquarters, was also the scene of heavy fighting in 1956.

Rákóczi út, terminates at Baross Square and is crowned by the grandiose imperial-looking **Keleti (East) Railway Station,** built in 1884 and considered Europe's most modern until well into this century. Its neo-Renaissance facade, which resembles a gateway, is flanked by statues of two British inventors and railway pioneers, James Watt and George Stephenson. The two entrance halls are decorated with murals by Károly Lotz, but its interior has recently become a dormitory for the homeless victims of Hungary's economic restructuring.

Doubling back on Rákóczi út to the Emke crossing at Blaha Lujza Square, you can now go either left or right on Pest's Great Ring Road, the **Nagy körút,** laid out at the end of the 19th century in a wide semicircle anchored to the Danube at both ends; an arm of the river was covered over to create this 35-meter (114-feet) wide thoroughfare. The large apartment buildings on both sides also date from this era. Along with theaters, stores, and cafés, they form a boulevard unique in Europe for its "unified eclecticism" which blends a variety of historic styles into a harmonious whole. Its entire length of almost 4½ kilometers (2¾ miles) from Margaret Bridge to Petőfi Bridge is traversed by trams no. 4 and 6, but strolling it in stretches is also a good way to experience the hustle and bustle of downtown Budapest.

As with its smaller counterpart, the Kis (Little) Körút, the Great Ring Road comprises variously named streets. The sector to your left (if you're facing Buda) is called József körút, and your exploration of it begins with the neo-Renaissance building of the Technology Institute, built in 1887–89.

Farther along, on the left-hand side, is the pleasant Rákóczi tér, known as Calf Square until 1884 because it was the meat marketplace; it is now dominated by a handsome beige brick Market Hall built in 1897 with 400 stands.

⑤ At the corner of Üllői út, where the Great Ring Road becomes Ferenc körút, stands a templelike structure that is indeed a shrine to Hungarian Art Nouveau. It is the **Iparművészeti Múzeum** (Museum of Applied and Decorative Arts), and in front of it, drawing-pen in hand, sits a statue of its creator, Ödön Lechner, Hungary's master of Art Nouveau. Opened in the millennial year of 1896, it was only the third museum of its kind in Europe. Its dome of tiles is crowned by a majolica lantern from the same source: the Zsolnay ceramic works in Pecs. Inside its central hall are playfully swirling whitewashed double-decker Moorish-style galleries and arcades. The museum, which collects and studies objects of interior decoration and use, has five departments: furniture, textiles, goldsmithery, ceramics, and everyday objects. *Üllői út 33–37, tel. 361/1175–222 or 1175–635. Admission: 20 Ft. adults, 10 Ft. children. Open Tues.–Sun. 10–6.*

Ferenc körút runs from Üllői út to Petőfi Bridge and was once known as Mill Street, the main artery of the German Quarter (Ferencváros or Franzstadt) until the great flood of 1838 swept away all but 19 of its 500 mud-brick houses. It ends at Boráros ter, a major transportation hub and terminus of the suburban train to the Csepel factory district.

Back when you were at the Emke crossing, if you had turned to the right, you would have been traveling along **Erzsébet (Elizabeth) körút** (formerly Lenin körút). Beyond its intersection with Király utca (King Street, formerly Majakovszkij utca), it's now Teréz (Theresa) körút. Just around the Emke corner, at Erzsébet körút 9–11, is the New York Palace, a striking 1894–95 millennium promotion designed by Alajos Hauszmann for an American insurance company.

Time Out The most imposing part of the New York Palace is its downstairs, multilevel **New York Coffeehouse** (tel. 361/1223–849), also known as **Café Hungaria:** a medley of brass and glass, silver and gold, marble and mirrors, animated frescoes and twisted columns, Venetian chandeliers and richly carved galleries. For nearly a century it has been a meeting place for artists, authors, and particularly for journalists, who, at its grand opening, threw its key into the Danube so that it would have to stay open day and night (the hours are now 10 AM to midnight). Along the paneled, brass-railed bar are sketches and caricatures of celebrities whose names seem to have been given to half the streets in the area. At the turn of the century, a plate of cold cuts served only to writers and journalists at a very low price, was known as the "writer's special." The headwaiter, "Uncle Gyula," not only provided ink and paper but was also known to extend credit. There are no longer any bargains here, but there is a money changer on the premises. Hot meals can be erratic, but the pastries and coffee are impeccable.

At Erzsébet körút 29–33 is the **Madach Theatre,** the city's third-largest, and a few doors up is the Hotel Royal. Right after Erzsébet becomes Teréz körút, the reason for the name change appears: the Baroque **Terézvárosi Romai-Katolikus Templom** (Theresa Town Parish Church) with Classical altars and finely proportioned choir designed by Mihály Pollack. Beyond the busy Octogon crossing with Andrássy út and the beautifully re-done Hotel Béke Radisson, Teréz körút ends at the **Nyugati (West) Railway Station.** Designed by the French architect Auguste de Serres, it was built between 1874 and 1877 on the site where the first Hungarian train departed on July 15, 1846. Its iron-laced glass hall is in complete contrast to—and much more modern than—the newer Keleti (East) Station.

The final stretch of the Great Ring Road is **Szent István (St. Stephen) körút,** with the **Vígszínház** (Comedy Theatre) at No. 14. Designed in neo-Baroque style by the Viennese imperial architectural team of Fellner and Helmer and built in 1895–86, it twinkles with just a tiny, playful anticipation of Art Nouveau and a happy ending to this marathon stroll through the sprawling heart of Pest.

Tour 4: Óbuda

Until its unification with Buda and Pest in 1872 to form the city of Budapest, **Óbuda** (the name means Old Buda) was a separate town that used to be the main settlement; now it is usually thought of as a suburb. Although the vast new apartment blocks of Budapest's biggest housing project are what first strike the eye, the historic core of Óbuda has been preserved in its entirety as an ancient monument.

Óbuda is easily reached by car, bus, or streetcar via the Arpad Bridge from Pest or by the HÉV suburban railway from Batthyány tér to Árpád hid. Behind the new Thermal Hotel Aquincum is a serene Baroque gem built in the 18th century by the Zichy family (which owned all of Óbuda at the time): the **Óbuda Parish Church** (1744–49), which houses the tomb of Pál Zichy (1723) and many objects from the nearby Kiscelli Monastery.

Across the main road leading off the bridge is an oval building built in 1785 called the **Deglomeratorium,** or Silk-Winding Building. Its two-story workshop and interior gallery have been restored as a monument to the textile industry. There is usually an exhibition of the making of silk.

The center of today's Óbuda is **Flórián tér,** where Roman ruins were first discovered when the foundations of a house were dug in 1778. Two centuries later, careful excavations were carried out during the reconstruction of the square. Between 1981 and 1984, 48 rooms of Roman military baths known as *Thermae Maiores* were excavated, and some of them were formed into an open-air museum that can be viewed by those taking the pedestrian underpass to cross the square. Besides pools and steam chambers, the baths also had rooms for rest and recreation, a promenade, and a temple dedicated to the nymphs of healing. *Tel. 1804–650. Admission: 20 Ft. Open daily 10–6. Guided tours in English and German.*

If you stroll southward toward the center of Buda along Pacsirtamező utca, at No. 63 you'll find the **Roman Castrum Museum,** which is dedicated to relics and ruins from the residential district where merchants and craftsmen as well as some of the more prosperous Roman officers lived. Farther south, at the busy junction where Pacsirtamező utca (formerly Korvin Ottó utca) meets Bécsi út, is a Roman **Military Amphitheater** that held some 16,000 people. It probably dates to the 2nd century. At 144 yards in diameter, this oval arena was one of Europe's largest. A block of dwellings called the Round House was later built by the Romans above the amphitheater; massive stone walls found in the Round House's cellar were actually parts of the amphitheater. Below the amphitheater are the cells where prisoners and lions were held while awaiting confrontation.

From here, climb eastward to the **Kiscelli Museum** on Remethegy (Hermit's Hill). This plain Baroque building was built between 1744 and 1760 as a Trinitarian monastery with funds donated by the Zichy family. After the order was dissolved, the building was used as a barracks and a hospital. Later it was purchased by a Viennese furniture manufacturer, and, after his death in 1935, it became city property. Today it is a museum housing the interior of the old Golden Lion Pharmacy, 18th- and 19th-century printing presses, temporary exhibitions of art and local history, and the fine-arts collection of the Budapest History Museum. It specializes in painting, engravings, and sculptures related to the history of the city; it also houses three or four major works of each artist who played an important role in the cultural life of Budapest. Its 20th-century collection is small but valuable. *Kiscelli út 108, tel. 1888–560. Admission: 20 Ft. Open May–Nov., Tues.–Sun. 10–6; Dec.–Apr., Tues.–Sun. 10–4.*

Follow Kiscelli út downhill to Flórián tér and continue toward the Danube; take a left at Hidlo utca or Szentélek tér to enter Óbuda's old main square, **Fő tér.** This area has been spruced up in recent years, and there are now several good restaurants and interesting museums in and around the Baroque **Zichy Mansion,** which has become a neighborhood cultural center. Among the most popular offerings are the summer concerts in the courtyard and the Monday-evening jazz concerts.

One wing of the Zichy Mansion is taken up by the **Budai Helytörténeti Múzeum** (Óbuda Local History Museum); permanent exhibitions here include one devoted to the district of Békásmegyer and another that recreates the workshop of master cooper Simon Tóbiás. *Zichy Mansion, Fő tér 1, tel. 1804–020. Admission: 20 Ft. Open Tues.–Fri. 2–6, Sat.–Sun. 10–6.*

Another wing of the Zichy Mansion houses the **Lajos Kassák Memorial Museum,** which honors the literary and artistic works of a pioneer of the Hungarian avant-garde. *Zichy Mansion, Fő tér 1, tel. 1687–021. Admission: 10 Ft. Open Tues.–Sun. 10–6.*

For information about the Roman settlement **Aquincum** and the area north of Budapest, *see* Chapter 3.

What to See and Do with Children

Budapest has two zoos that provide excellent diversions for children (and adults) weary of museums and churches. At the Budakeszi **Vadaspark** deer, wild sheep, wild boar, and birds (most indigenous to Hungary) can be seen in a lovely natural setting. *Take bus No. 22 to Koranyi stop. Open daily 10–6.*

The **Budapest Zoo** in Varosliget Park cares for a more exotic variety of animals, including hippos, a favorite of local youngsters. *XIV Allatkerti korut 6–12, behind Heroes Square. Open May–Sept., Mon., Tues., and Thurs.–Sun. 9–dusk.*

Next to the Budapest Zoo is **Vidám Park,** the city's main amusement park, open spring through fall. It has rides, game rooms, and a scenic railway. There are some rides for preschoolers. Next to the main park is a separate smaller amusement park for toddlers. *Városliget. Open Apr.–Sept., daily 10–8; Sept.–Mar., daily 10–7.*

The 12-kilometer (7-mile) **Pioneer Railway** (operated in Communist days by the Young Pioneers) runs from Szechenyihegy to Huvosvolgy. Departures are from Szechenyihegy, which you can reach by taking the delightful cogwheel railway from the station opposite Hotel Budapest (Szilagyi Erzsébet fasor 47).

Even non-Hungarian-speaking children are amused by the antics at Budapest's two **puppet theaters: Babszinhaz** (V Jokai ter 10) and **Allami Babszinhaz** (VI Andrassy ut 69).

A new **circus** (Nagy Cirkusz, XIV Allatkerti körút 7) comes to Budapest every six or eight weeks. Tickets can be purchased in advance at VI Andrassy ut 61.

Off the Beaten Track

A *libegő* (chair lift) will take you to the highest point in Budapest, the **Jánoshegy** (Janos Hill), where you can climb a lookout tower for the best view of the city. *Take bus no. 158 from Moszkva tér to the last stop, Zugligeti út. Admission: 20 Ft. Open May 15–Sept. 15, daily 9–5.*

Sightseeing Checklists

This list includes both attractions covered in the preceding tours and additional ones described here for the first time.

Historic Buildings and Sights

Andrassy út (*see* Tour 3)
Árpád Bridge (Árpádhíd, *see* Tour 2)
Batthyány Palace (*see* Tour 1)
Batthyány tér (*see* Tour 1)
Central Market Hall (*see* Tour 3)
Chain Bridge (Széchenyi-lanchíd, *see* Tour 2)
Citadella (*see* Tour 1)
City Hall (Városház, *see* Tour 3)
City Park (Városliget, *see* Tour 3)
Corvin tér (*see* Tour 1)
Deák tér (*see* Tour 3)
Deglomeratorium (*see* Tour 4)
Egyetem tér (*see* Tour 3)
Elizabeth Bridge (Erzsébethíd, *see* Tour 2)

Erszébet tér (*see* Tour 3)
Fisherman's Bastion (Halászbástya, *see* Tour 1)
Fő tér, Óbuda (*see* Tour 4)
Fő utca (*see* Tour 1)
Gellért Hill (Gellért-hegy, *see* Tour 1)
Gellért Hotel and Baths (*see* Tour 1)
Great Ring Road (Nagy korut, *see* Tour 3)
Gresham Building (*see* Tour 3)
Hősök tere (Heroes' Square, *see* Tour 3)
Janos Hill (Janoshegy, *see* Off the Beaten Track)
Kálvin tér (*see* Tour 3)
Kapisztrán tér (*see* Tour 1)
Király Baths (*see* Tour 1)
Kis (Inner) körút (*see* Tour 3)
Klotild and Matild buildings (*see* Tour 3)
Kodály körönd (*see* Tour 3)
Korzó (*see* Tour 3)
Labyrinth of Buda Castle (*see* Tour 1)
Liberty Bridge (Szabadsághíd, *see* Tour 2)
Liberty Square (Szabadság tér, *see* Tour 3)
Margaret Bridge (Margithíd, *see* Tour 2)
Margaret Island (Margit-sziget, *see* Tour 2)
Nagy (Outer) körút (*see* Tour 3)
Paris Arcades (*see* Tour 3)
Parliament (Országház, *see* Tour 3)
People's Stadium (Népstadion, *see* Tour 3)
Petőfi Bridge (*see* Tour 2)
Rác Baths (*see* Tour 1)
Rákóczi út (*see* Tour 3)
Roman Military Amphitheater (*see* Tour 4)
Roosevelt tér (*see* Tour 3)
Rose Hill (Rózsadomb, *see* Tour 1)
Royal Palace (Királyi Palota, *see* Tour 1)
Rudas Baths (*see* Tour 1)
Sports Hall (Sportcsarnok, *see* Tour 3)
Stag House (Szarvas-haz, *see* Tour 1)
Szechenyi Baths (*see* Tour 3)
Szechenyi National Library (*see* Tour 1)
Szilágyi Dezső tér (*see* Tour 1)
Tabán (*see* Tour 1)
Thermae Maiores (*see* Tour 4)
Váci utca (*see* Tour 3)
Várhegy (Castle Hill, *see* Tour 1)
Vienna Gate Square (Bécsi kapu tér, *see* Tour 1)
Vigadó tér (*see* Tour 3)
Vörösmarty tér (*see* Tour 3)
Zichy Mansion (*see* Tour 4)

Churches and Temples
Capuchin Church (*see* Tour 1)
Florian Chapel (Szent Florian-kapolna, *see* Tour 1)
Franciscan Church (*see* Tour 3)
Great Synagogue (*see* Tour 3)
Greek Orthodox Church (*see* Tour 3)
Inner City Parish Church (Belvárosi plébánia-templom, *see* Tour 3)
Lutheran Church (*see* Tour 3)
Matthias Church (Mátyás templom, *see* Tour 1)
Medieval Synagogue (*see* Tour 1)
Óbuda Parish Church (*see* Tour 4)
St. Anne (Szent Anna-templom, *see* Tour 1)

St. Mary Magdalene (Mária Magdolna-templom, *see* Tour 1)
St. Roch Chapel (*see* Tour 3)
St. Stephen's Basilica (Szent István Bazilika, *see* Tour 3)
St. Theresa (Terézvárosi Romai-Katolikus templom, *see* Tour 3)
Serbian Orthodox Church (*see* Tour 3)
Slovak Lutheran Church (*see* Tour 3)
Tabán Parish Church (Tabán plébánia-templom, *see* Tour 1)
University Church (*see* Tour 3)

Museums and   **Agricultural Museum** (Mezőgazdasági Múzeum, *see* Tour 3)
Galleries   **Art Gallery** (Műcsarnok, *see* Tour 3)
Budapest History Museum (Budapesti Történeti Múzeum, *see* Tour 1)
Ferenc Hopp Museum of Eastern Asiatic Arts (*see* Tour 3)
Golden Eagle Pharmacy Museum (Arany Sas Patika, *see* Tour 1)
Hungarian National Gallery (Magyar Nemzeti Galéria, *see* Tour 1)
Hungarian National Museum (Magyar Nemzeti Múzeum, *see* Tour 3)
Kiscelli Museum (*see* Tour 4)
Lajos Kassák Memorial Museum (*see* Tour 4)
Liszt Museum (*see* Tour 3)
Lutheran Museum (Evangélikus Múzeum, *see* Tour 3)
Museum of Applied and Decorative Arts (Iparmüvészeti Múzeum, *see* Tour 3)
Museum of Commerce and Catering (Kereskedelmi és Vendéglátóipari Múzeum, *see* Tour 1)
Museum of Domestic Culture (Lakásmúzeum) features regional pottery, carvings, and textiles. *Fő tér 4, Óbuda, tel. 1803–340. Admission: 10 Ft. Open Tues.–Sun. 10–6.*
Museum of Ethnography (Néprajzi Múzeum, *see* Tour 3)
Museum of Fine Arts (Szépmüvészeti Múzeum, *see* Tour 3)
Museum of the Hungarian Army (Hadtörténeti Intézet és Múzeum, *see* Tour 1)
Museum of Hungarian Telephone Technology (*see* Tour 1)
Museum of Medical History (Semmelweis Orvostörténeti Múzeum, *see* Tour 1)
Museum of Music History (Zenetörténeti Múzeum, *see* Tour 1)
Museum of Recent History (Legujabbkori Történeti Múzeum, *see* Tour 1)
National Jewish Museum (*see* Tour 3)
Óbuda Local History Museum (Budai Helytörténeti Múzeum, *see* Tour 4)
Postal Museum (Postamúzeum, *see* Tour 3)
Roman Castrum Museum (*see* Tour 4)
Transport Museum (*see* Tour 3)
Varga Gallery houses the works of the contemporary Hungarian sculptor Imre Varga; the artist often receives visitors in the museum on Saturday. *Laktanya tér 6, Óbuda. Admission: 10 Ft. Open Tues.–Sun. 10–6.*
Vasarely Museum in Óbuda offers a good chronological sampling of the work of Victor Vasareli (born in 1908 in the city of Pécs), the founder of Op Art. Temporary exhibitions are often devoted to other expatriate Hungarian artists. *Szentélek tér 6, Óbuda, tel. 1840–640 or 1887–661. Admission: 10 Ft. Open Tues.–Sun. 10–6.*

Statues and   **Attila Jozsef statue** (*see* Tour 3)
Monuments   **Empress Elizabeth statue** (*see* Tour 2)
Jozsef Bem statue (*see* Tour 1)

Lajos Kossuth statue (*see* Tour 3)
Liberation Memorial (*see* Tour 1)
Mihaly Karolyi statue (*see* Tour 3)
Millenial Monument (*see* Tour 3)
Nereides Fountain (*see* Tour 3)
Prince Eugene of Savoy statue (*see* Tour 1)
Tomb of Gül Baba (*see* Tour 1)
Trinity Column (*see* Tour 1)

Theaters and Academy of Fine Arts (*see* Tour 3)
Concert Halls Castle Theater (Várszínház, *see* Tour 1)
Children's Theater (*see* Tour 3)
Comedy Theater (Vigszinház, *see* Tour 3)
Ferenc Erkel Theater (*see* Tour 3)
Liszt Academy of Music (*see* Tour 3)
Madach Theater (*see* Tour 3)
Opera House (*see* Tour 3)
Puppet Theater (*see* Tour 3)
Vigadó Concert Hall (*see* Tour 3)

Shopping

Shopping Districts The principal upscale shopping district in **Pest** is the **pedestrian zone** on and around **Váci utca** between the Elisabeth (Erzsébet) and Chain (Szechenyi-lanchid) bridges. For fashion, try the boutiques in the **World Trade Center** passage at Váci utca 19–21 or Fontana-Mode at No. 16. You'll find plenty of folk-art-and-souvenir shops, foreign-language bookshops, and classical-record shops in and around Váci utca, but a visit to some of the smaller, more typically Hungarian shops on **Erzsébet** and **Teréz boulevards** (formerly Lenin Körút) may prove more interesting.

Department Stores Department stores along Rákóczi út include **Verseny** at No. 12, **Csillag** at Nos. 20-22, and **Lotto** at No. 36. **Skala Metro** (Marx tér 1–2), opposite the Nyugati (West) railroad station, is the newest and largest department store. Elsewhere downtown, another important fashion boutique is that of **Zsuzsa Lorincz** (Regiposta utca 14).

The **flea market** (*ecseri piac*), some way out on Nagykőrösi utca 156 (take bus no. 58 from Boráros tér), stocks antiques, clothes, lamps, and other Hungarian items.

Specialty Stores
Antiques For antiques, try **Sallay** (Lengyel Gyula utca 6), **Kruj** (Néphadsereg utca 28), **Antiquity** (Néphadsereg utca 32), **Csikos** (Néphadsereg utca 30), **Párizsi Tango** (Párizsi utca 6/b), or **Polgar and Tarsa** (József körút 15). Three **state stores** (Kossuth Lajos utca 1–3, Ferencziek tere 3, and Bécsi utca 1–3) also carry a good selection.

Books You can purchase English-language books at **Central Secondhand Bookshop** (V Múzeum körút 15), **Idegennyelvu Konyvesbolt** (Foreign Bookstore, V Petőfi Sándor utca 2, in passageway), **Konyvert Teka** (Honvéd utca 5), **Interbright** (XII Tarsay Vilnos utca 13), and **Libri** (V Váci utca 32).

China, Crystal, and Porcelain Hungary is famous for its **Herend** china (hand-painted in the village of Herend) and **Zsolnay** porcelain. Good selections can be found in the shops in the Forum, Hilton, and Duna Intercontinental hotels. Hungarian and Czechoslovakian **crystal** is also considerably less expensive here than in the United States.

Two recommended sources are: the **Crystal Shop** (V Váci utca 9) and **Haas & Czjzek** (VI Bajcsy-Zsilinszky út 23).

Folk Art   One of the best places to go for **folk-art clothing** is the gift shop in the **Forum** hotel. Handmade articles are also often sold by Transylvanian women standing along Vaci utca, near the tram at Vigado ter, or in the larger metro stations. Other types of **folk art**—cabinets, jewelry boxes, woodcarvings, embroidery—can be purchased at **Hollo Muhely** (V Vitkovics utca 12) and **Folkart Studio** (V Kálvin tér 5). Blouses, tablecloths, carvings, ceramics, and painted plates are available at the **Folkart Centrum** (Váci utca 14). Across the river near Buda Castle, try **Judit Folklore** (I, Orszaghaz utca 12).

Leather   Leather goods are reasonably priced in Hungary. Several shops on Váci utca sell gloves, and many department stores offer a wide selection of leather clothing and accessories.

Music   **Classical records** and **tapes** of excellent quality are a good buy in Hungary; they are often packaged with explanatory text or a libretto in English. Good places to look are **Rozsavolgyi** (Marinelli tér), **Interdisc** at the Hotel Duna InterContinental (tel. 361/1184–032), **Hungaroton** (Vörösmarty tér 1, tel. 361/1176–222), and **Amadeus** (Szende Pal utca 1).

Sports and Fitness

Participants Sports

Golf   The **Budapest Golf Club** is at Kisoroszi on Szentendre Island north of the city. Contact the Budapest office at Bécsi utca 5 for information (tel. 361/117–6025). You can also make reservations for golf games at the **Budapest Hilton** (tel. 361/175–1000).

Health and Fitness Clubs   The **Diadem Fitness Club** (also known as Cleo; VI, Lovolde tér 4, tel. 361/1221–204, 205, or 206) is open 24 hours a day. The **Margit Island Tennis Club** (*see* Tennis, *below*) also has a Nautilus gymnasium with a sauna. Pest's new **Hotel Helia** (tel. 361/1298–650) has an excellent swimming/health club complex that nonguests can use for under $10 a day. You can arrange to play **squash** at **Marczibanyi teri Muvelodesi Központ** (II, Marczibanyi tér 5/a, tel. 361/1359–917). The **Duna InterContinental**, the **Atrium Hyatt**, and the **Forum** have good facilities, but they're only for guests.

Jogging   **Margaret Island** and, on the Pest waterfront, the **Korzo** (Corso) promenade are level and inviting; the hills of Buda are not. The **City Park**, near Heroes' Square, is a good place for a run or walk.

Spas and Thermal Baths

Caszar Baths (II, Frankel Leo út 17–19, tel. 361/115–4680). This spring, near the famous Roman military road, is mentioned in the earliest written record of the Hungarian language. ORFI, the National Institute for Rheumatism and Physiotherapy (Frankel Leo utca 35, tel. 361/115–4680) uses the waters of Caszar Baths.

Gellért Spa Hotel (XI, Szent Gellért tér 1, tel. 361/185–2200) is the oldest Hungarian spa hotel; its hot springs have supplied baths for nearly 2,000 years.

Király Baths (II, Fő utca 84, tel. 361/115–3000). This establishment was built in the 16th century by the Turkish pasha of Buda.

Lukács Baths (II, Frankel Leó út 25–29, tel. 361/115–4280) adjoins the Caszar spa (*see above*) and benefits from the same source, which dates from the Bronze Age and Roman times.

Rác Baths (I, Hadnagy utca 8–10, tel. 361/156–1322) is a small bath facility tucked away at the foot of Gellért Hill near the Erzsébet bridge. Its waters contain alkaline salts and other minerals.

Rudas Medicinal Baths (I, Döbrentei tér 9, tel. 361/156–1322). This facility's highly fluoridated waters have been known for 1,000 years.

Széchenyi Baths (XIV, Állatkerti körút 11, tel. 361/121–0310), dating from 1876, are in a beautiful neo-Baroque building in the middle of the city-park green belt. This is one of the biggest spas in Europe.

The **Thermal Hotel** (XIII, Margitsziget, tel. 361/111–1000) offers a spa in an especially attractive location on Margaret Island. Guests at the adjoining Ramada Grand Hotel can use the Thermal Hotel spa.

The **Thermal Hotel Aquincum** (III, Arpad fejedelem utja 26, tel. 361/112–1000) and the **Thermal Hotel Helia** (XIII, Karpat utca 62, tel. 361/129–8650) are the newest spa hotels in Budapest; both opened in the last two years.

Dining

Eating out in Budapest can be a real treat and should provide you with some of the best value for money of any European capital. Meats, rich sauces, and creamy desserts predominate, but the more health-conscious will also find salads, even out of season. There is a good selection of restaurants, from the grander establishments that echo the imperial past of the Habsburg era to the less expensive spots favored by locals. In addition to restaurants (*vendeglo*), there are also self-service restaurants (*önkiszolgáló étterem*), snack bars (*bisztró* or *étel bár*), buffets (*büfé*), cafés (*eszpresszó*), bars (*drinkbár*), and pastry shops (*cukrászda*).

Highly recommended restaurants in each price category are indicated by a star ★.

Category	Cost*
Very Expensive	over 1,200 Ft.
Expensive	1,000 Ft.–1,200 Ft.
Moderate	600 Ft.–1,000 Ft.
Inexpensive	under 600 Ft.

*per person, including appetizer, entrée, and dessert but excluding drinks, and 10%–15% service

Very Expensive

★ **Alabárdos.** As medieval as its name, which means "halberdier" (the wielder of that ancient weapon, the halberd), this vaulted wooden room in a 400-year-old Gothic house across from the Matthias Church and Budapest Hilton is widely regarded as one of Hungary's best restaurants. It has only nine tables, though in summer a courtyard garden doubles its capacity. The impeccable service, flowery decor, quiet music, and overriding discretion make this an excellent place for a serious business meal. Specialties are Hungarian meats and steaks with goose-liver trimmings. Start with *palócleves,* a sour-creamy soup of beef, potatoes, and green beans. The room's lights go out every time the flambéed mixed grill is delivered; if you don't like to be the center of attention, try the filet mignon in green pepper sauce, also flambéed but without the pyrotechnics. The goose-liver-stuffed pork cutlets light their own fire, thanks to *lecsó,* a spicy mix of tomato, paprika, and onions. Desserts include homemade apple and cherry strudels, *somló* (a kind of sponge cake soaked in chocolate sauce and whipped cream), and *Posztobányi pudding* (a fruity chocolate pudding served with sour cherries). *I, Országház utca 2, tel. 361/1560–851. Jacket and tie advised. Reservations required. AE, DC, MC, V. Dinner only. Closed Sun.*

Gundel. This is the shrine where Hungary's famous dessert, *Gundel palacsinta* (Gundel pancakes), was invented around the turn of the century by the restaurant's second owner, Károly Gundel. Filled with walnuts, lemon rind, raisins, and orange peel and coated with chocolate sauce, the crepes are flamed in rum at the table—and they never disappoint. The earlier courses are hardly a mere prelude, however; the soups (like the pheasant consommé with quail's egg) are as light as the desserts. The main dishes are delicious, particularly the sirloin fricassee, which is braised with goose liver, white asparagus tips, and scrambled eggs; and the duck steak Budapest style. Service is efficient and friendly. This austere place, with plain wooden paneling and clusters of chandeliers, occupies a palatial mansion in the City Park, a 15-minute ride by subway or car from downtown Pest. There is a special room for groups upstairs, so the large main dining room is never noisy at lunch; if you want quiet at night, ask for a table away from the Gypsy music. In summer, tables are set up in the garden. At press time, Gundel had been purchased by American entrepreneurs George Lang and Ronald Lauder, who closed the restaurant for thorough renovations. The new, restored Gundel was scheduled to open in mid-May 1992. *XIV, Állatkerti út 2, tel. 361/1221–022 or 361/1213–550. Reservations advised. Jacket and tie advised. AE, DC, MC, V.*

★ **Légrádi Testvérek.** This is perhaps the most prestigious and certainly one of the most luxurious Hungarian restaurants in Budapest. Prompt, unobtrusive service is provided at candle-lit, lace-covered tables set with Herend china. Hors d'oeuvres include smoked salmon, caviar, terrines of foie gras and fish, and steak tartare. Standard but beautifully presented entrées range from chateaubriand to wild boar. The game dishes are highly recommended. *V, Magyar utca 23, tel. 361/118–6804. Reservations required. Jacket and tie advised. No credit cards.*

★ **Paradiso.** Hungarian nouvelle cuisine was born to high praise in 1985 in this small restaurant in a private house high on a hill in Buda. Trained in France, Switzerland, Germany, New York,

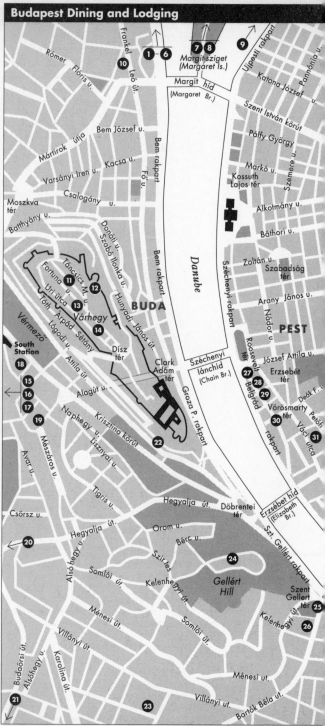

Dining

Alabárdos, **13**
Arany Hordó, **14**
Aranymókus
Kertvendéglő, **17**
Baroque, **38**
Duna-Corso, **29**
Fortuna, **11**
Gundel, **41**
Kaltenberg, **35**
Kehli, **5**
Kis Buda, **10**
Légrádi Testvérek, **34**
Márvány
Menyasszony, **19**
Paradiso, **16**
Postakocsi, **2**
Sipos Halászkert, **3**
Svejk, **37**
Szeged, **26**
Tabáni Kakas, **22**
Vadászkert, **4**
Vasmacska, **1**

Lodging

Aquincum, **6**
Astoria, **32**
Atrium Hyatt, **27**
Béke Radisson, **39**
Buda Penta, **18**
Budapest Hilton, **12**
Citadella, **24**
Duna
InterContinental, **30**
Erzsébet, **33**
Flamenco, **23**
Forum, **28**
Gellért, **25**
Grand Hotel
Hungaria, **40**
Helia, **9**
Nemzeti, **36**
Novotel, **20**
Panorama Hotels-
Bungalows, **15**
Ramada Grand
Hotel, **8**
Taverna, **31**
Thermal, **7**
Wien, **21**

Budapest Dining and Lodging

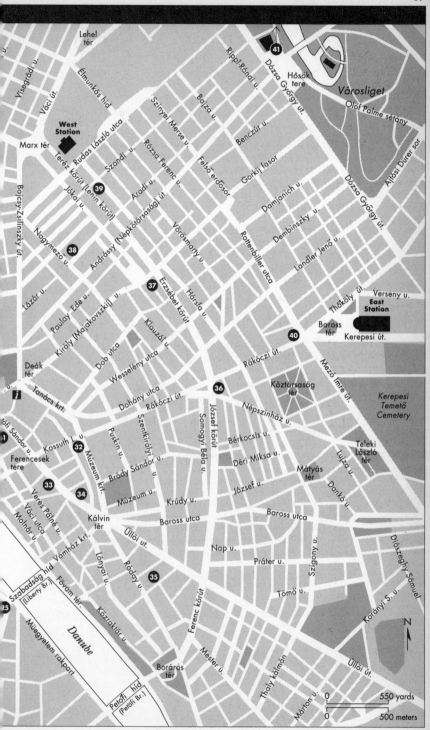

and Chicago, Chef János Cseh is constantly inventing new dishes. Memorable creations have included caviar pancakes with white-onion sauce; the Neptune Fantasy, a starfish of roasted trout and salmon strips in white wine sauce, accompanied by little shells filled with onion, cabbage, crayfish, and mussels; and a hot sour-cherry strudel. Hungarian wines are poured by the glass, enabling the staff to recommend the right accompaniment to each course. The main dining area is a living room with theatrical red curtains, a green ceramic stove, and, on the walls, a many-splendored Persian carpet competing with a 200-year-old painting of a jolly Last Supper. A pianist plays discreetly at night; if you want more privacy, try for the small room in back with two tables. *XII, Istenhegyi út 40/a, tel. 361/ 1531–988. Reservations required. Jacket and tie advised. AE, DC, MC, V. Closed Sun.*

Expensive

Arany Hordó. True to its name, the Golden Barrel, this 14th-century building has a beerhouse on the ground floor. The cellar has a wine tavern, but the real attraction is the first-class restaurant on the second floor. The local specialty is *fogas*, a fish from Lake Balaton. There is Gypsy music in the evening. *I, Tárnok utca 16, tel. 361/1566–765. Reservations advised for restaurant. Dress: casual. AE, DC, MC, V.*

Baroque. This small and intimate restaurant offers dishes adapted from 17th- and 18th-century recipes. The warm atmosphere is enhanced by striking reproductions of Baroque furniture and piped-in Baroque music. *VI, Mozsar utca 12, tel. 361/ 1318–942. Reservations advised. Dress: casual but neat. No credit cards.*

Fortuna. This appealing wooden complex (restaurant, tavern, and nightclub), connecting three medieval houses across from the Hilton, is included mainly because Hungarians like to be taken here—although many Americans like the atmosphere and food, too. But the service can be slapdash and negligent, the Gypsy band insistent and amateurish, and the goose liver undistinguished. The flaming Gundel pancakes are often overdosed with rum and hot chocolate syrup. Nonetheless, it can be a good setting for a filling meal—either in the restaurant, with its red-plush fabric walls, or the rustic, wooden tavern—as long as you get the waiters and musicians to leave you alone. The offerings in the tavern are less expensive than those in the main restaurant. *I, Hess András tér 4, tel. 361/1756–857, 361/ 1756–175. Reservations advised. Dress: casual but neat. AE, DC, MC, V in restaurant and nightclub; no credit cards in tavern.*

Postakocsi. In this cavernous cellar under the main square of Óbuda (Old Buda) stands the public stagecoach that set out on the first journey from here to Vienna in 1752. It serves as the bar of this large restaurant, which is decorated with saddles, horseshoes, and other equestrian doodads. The Hungarian menu includes specialties from Transylvania such as stuffed sirloin of beef. Goose liver is everywhere—inside mushrooms, in the dressings and secret stuffings of the steaks, fried with French fries, roasted with apples, and in the Hungarian goose-liver stew. Gypsy musicians wander from room to room, making this more a place for fun than serious talk. For relative peace and quiet, try the folk-art-furnished Transylvanian Room with its heavy, violin-shaped wooden chairs. *III, Fő tér*

2, tel. 361/1687–801. Reservations advised. Jacket and tie advised. AE, DC, MC, V.

Vasmacska. Everything is shipshape in this nautical garden-restaurant (its name means "anchor"), located a few steps from the Óbuda shipyard whose workers and sailors it started serving around 1856. The wood-paneled main dining room is furnished like a combination of captain's cabin and ship's saloon; the wine-cellar tavern slopes at a rakish tilt, and there's a bowling alley in the beer hall. Despite the seafaring motif, fish dishes don't predominate, though the catfish in red wine is highly recommended. The name of the game here is game: flaming saddle of deer with three sauces; roast Transylvanian wild boar with juniper sauce. For dessert, try the peach pancakes in vanilla sauce. The inn was renovated and enlarged in 1985 to accommodate Budapest's middle-class prop-jet set and group tours, but it still has many quiet crannies for business conversation. *III, Laktanya utca 3–5, tel. 361/1887–123. Reservations advised. Dress: casual. AE, DC, MC, V.*

Moderate

Aranymókus Kertvendéglő. If you can't get into Paradiso (*see above*), don't despair. Directly across the street is this folksy Hungarian garden restaurant (the Golden Squirrel) offering the kind of food that goes well with beer. There are no bones to pick with (or find) in the fiery carp soup, except that a cold drink must be standing by. Platters overflow with beef, veal, game, liver, and fish; the baked potatoes are huge. Fillet of fogas in crayfish and dill sauce tastes better than it looks, and the poppy-seed pancakes in coconut butter taste better than they sound—they'll send you waddling home happy. There's a good salad bar, too. Best of all is the atmosphere generated by the rustic wooden furniture and happy Hungarian diners. *XII, Istenhegyi út 25, tel. 361/1556–728. Reservations advised. Dress: casual. No credit cards. Closed Mon.*

★ **Duna-Corso.** One of Budapest's best-kept secrets is out. This stolid, family-oriented institution, which has long stood on the riverfront square dominated by the Vigadó concert hall, offers good, solid food at reasonable prices right in the center of Pest's luxury-hotel belt. Word of mouth, however, has spread Duna-Corso's fame, and now it's been discovered by foreign tourists. There's a German-language menu and, by the time you read this, there will probably be one in English. So far, neither price nor quality shows signs of changing for the worse. The bean and cabbage soups (laced with pork), duck with sauerkraut, and all kinds of liver (beef, pork, chicken, goose) are as simple and hearty as ever, and the service is still pokey and friendly. This noisy, bustling spot, where you're likely to wind up sharing a table with curious Hungarians, is no place for serious discussions, but it's wonderful for eating and enjoyment, and you won't feel lonely if you're by yourself. *V, Vigadó tér 3, tel. 361/1186–362 or 361/1180–913. Reservations sometimes possible. Dress: casual. No credit cards.*

★ **Kaltenberg.** This large brewery restaurant—with its vaulted red-brick ceiling, large wooden tables, gaslight-style lamps, and strings of pretzels and sausages hanging from the ceiling— looks as if it's been here forever, but it's barely five years old. The beer is made right here; take your choice of filtered *(HBH)* or cloudy unfiltered draft *(Ászok)*. Much of the food is Germanic (Bavarian cabbage soup, stuffed suckling pig), but there are

also Hungarian specialties (*hortobágyi* pancakes filled with
spicy meat, chestnut-and-chocolate dessert pancakes). Those
put off by the beerhall exterior will be charmed by the salad bar
and the exquisite raspberry desserts. The main room can be
very noisy, but there are several smaller rooms, one of them is
soundproofed and is sometimes rented by politicians and diplo-
mats. *IX, Kinizsi utca 30–36, tel. 361/1189–792. Reservations
advised. Dress: casual. AE, DC, MC, V.*

Kis Buda. On the site of a 14th-century inn near the Buda end of
the Margaret Bridge is this small, romantic, candle-lit multilevel restaurant. Its goose liver and fish specialties are prepared with such imagination that it's sometimes better not to
probe. Asked why the veal cutlet Kis Buda style was so good,
the headwaiter replied, "Because we use fantasy. We cook it
with brains." Diners may prefer not to take the comment liter-
ally. In addition to an appealing and fairly extensive menu,
there are specials that the waiter will tell you about. A piano
and violin duo tune up at 7 PM, but the atmosphere is always
quiet and conducive to serious conversation. *II, Frankel Leó út
34, tel. 361/1152–244. Reservations required. Dress: casual but
neat. Credit cards expected soon. Closed Sun. dinner.*

Sipos Halászkert. Károly Sipos founded Budapest's best-
known fish restaurant, relocated and rebuilt here (after a fire)
in 1983 with stones from an 11th-century church that once
stood on this Óbuda site. It is now a folksy, meandering, farm-
house-and-garden complex of rooms with a red-and-black
hurdy-gurdy in the entranceway that guests can crank and
play. Each room is different—one hunter-style, with red carpeting and animal skins; one pub-style; one elegant. The fish
salad of carp, egg, and caviar will whet your appetite for an excellent fiery fish soup. The fish stew in red wine with farmer
cheese sauce is a superb main course. Waiters will recommend
the right Badacsony white wines and Kecskemét red wines.
Sipos also knows how to cook meat, pork, and poultry. *III, Fő
tér 6, tel. 361/1888–745. Reservations advised. Dress: casual.
AE, DC, MC, V.*

Svejk. Tibor Sipos, a Slovak from Bratislava, has created the
best of six Czechoslovakian restaurants in town: Svejk, named
after the antihero of Jaroslav Hašek's novel *The Good Soldier
Schweik*. In a bourgeois corner of downtown Pest, Svejk features Czech combinations of pork, dumplings, and sauerkraut,
all rendered with a lighter and spicier Slovak touch and a slight
Hungarian influence. A Slovak specialty, stuffed tenderloin
Bratislava (breaded fillet filled with mushrooms, cheese, and
ham), and Svejk cakes (fried potato gnocchi spiced with ham
and sausage) should be washed down with fast-flowing Pilsner
beer from the barrel. The jovial but subdued literary atmosphere (a long, masculine room in shades of brown, decorated
with Jósef Lada's illustrations from the novel) and cordial but
discreet service make Svejk a good locale for quiet, lingering
evening meals. *VII, Király (formerly, Majakovszkij) utca
59/b, tel. 361/1223–278. Reservations advised. Dress: casual.
No credit cards.*

Szeged. This is a traditional fish restaurant in Buda near the
Szabadság Bridge and Gellért Hill. Folk art covers the walls,
and there is Gypsy music in the evening. The fish soup is fiery.
*XI, Bartók Béla út 1, tel. 361/1251–268. Reservations accepted.
Dress: casual. No credit cards.*

Tabáni Kakas. Situated just below Castle Hill, this popular restaurant has a friendly atmosphere and specializes in large help-

ings of poultry dishes, particularly goose. A pianist plays and
sings in the evening. *I, Áttila út 27, tel. 361/1757–165. No reservations. Dress: casual. No credit cards.*

Vadászkert. Walking into this elegant restaurant in Óbuda is
like entering the genteel living room of the wine merchant to
whom the manor house belonged a century ago. Upstairs, the
Round Room, decorated in turn-of-the-century sepia tones
with a round table that seats 12–14, is excellent for large
groups celebrating special occasions; some of Hungary's recent
history was decided here. Downstairs is the Readberger beer
cellar, an arcaded catacomb with adequate privacy for those
who seek it, though there is Gypsy music at night. Specialties
include veal medallions Kalocsa style (in a sauce of paprika,
egg, and tomato) and steak smothered in shellfish, mushrooms,
and fruits. For dessert, try the pudding of apricots from Kecskemét, the fruit garden of Hungary's Great Plain. In the summer, you can sit in one of two gardens adorned with stuffed
game and birds. *III, Hídfő utca 16, tel. 361/1887–399. Reservations advised. Dress: casual but neat. No credit cards.*

Inexpensive

★ **Kehli.** Formerly known as Hídvendéglő (Bridge Inn), the Kehli
is on a hard-to-find street near the Óbuda end of the Árpád
Bridge, near the new Hotel Aquincum. It's well worth the
search, though. A small, paneled, sepia-tone inn with a garden
(which in the summer more than doubles the restaurant's capacity) and an old wooden wagon decked with flowers out front,
this is still a neighborhood tavern where locals like to hang out
after work. The food is appropriately hearty and heavy. This is
not the place for health food (only the Óbuda-style mixed salad
with sheep cheese might qualify); just reading the menu could
raise your cholesterol. Select from appetizers like carp soup,
smoky bean soup, fried button mushrooms stuffed with brains,
or hot bone marrow with garlic toast (all of which go well with
the tavern's fine beer), before moving on to goose livers with
mashed potatoes or fried turkey breast stuffed with cheese and
goose liver. One of the inn's memorable specialties is pork steak
Father Fido style and barbecue—a tender, garlicky slice of
pork accompanied by potatoes broiled in beer and assorted tomato pickles and hot peppers. If you can't manage the Szuper-
Kamikaze ice-cream dessert with whipped cream and fruit salad, try one of the lighter but delectable mixed strudels—
poppyseed-pumpkin, cherry-walnut, or hazelnut. *III, Mókus
utca 22, tel. 361/1886–938. Reservations advised. Dress: informal. No credit cards. Closed Sun.*

Márvány Menyasszony. Summer is the best time to appreciate
this spacious restaurant in a Buda back street near the Déli
(South) Railroad Station. It is popular with groups, probably
because its long wooden tables and benches give way to space
for dancing to Gypsy music. The food is nothing to write home
about, although the servings are substantial. *I Márvány utca
6, tel. 361/1756–165. Reservations accepted. Dress: casual. No
credit cards.*

Lodging

More of the major luxury and business-class hotel chains are represented in Budapest than in Vienna or in any of the Eastern European capitals. All of them, however, are Hungarian-run franchise operations with native touches that you won't find in any other Hilton or Ramada. And Budapest still has historic hotels that could be nowhere else in the world. (*See* the Lodging section of Staying in Hungary in Chapter 1 for more information.)

Addresses below are preceded by the district number (in Roman numerals) as well as the street address and Hungarian postal code. Districts V and VII are in downtown Pest; I is the main tourist district of Buda.

All prices are quoted in American dollars; foreigners must pay in hard currency in all hotels.

Highly recommended lodgings in each price category are indicated by a star ★.

Category	Cost*
Very Expensive	9,000 Ft.–14,000 Ft.
Expensive	7,000 Ft.–9,000 Ft.
Moderate	4,000 Ft.–7,000 Ft.
Inexpensive	1,500 Ft.–4,000 Ft.

*All prices are for a standard single room, including service, taxes, and (except for the Budapest Hilton), breakfast buffet.

Very Expensive

★ **Atrium Hyatt.** You might call this the Hyatt Smithsonian, for from the top of its 10-story atrium hangs a copy of a single-engine Hungarian airplane that flew over the Adriatic Sea in 1912. The spectacular interior—glass elevators, cascading water, a rain forest of tropical greenery, an open bar, and café—is surpassed only by the views across the Danube to the Royal Castle; rooms with a river view cost substantially more. Accommodations are modern but homey—you don't even feel like you're in a hotel—and suites have Thonet bentwood rocking chairs. The breakfast buffet features a *musli* table with grains, seeds, and cereals in addition to the more cholesterol-boosting spread. Well situated in the inner city near the Pest waterfront, the Hyatt and its facilities and amenities remain in the vanguard of the downtown hotels. *V, Roosevelt tér 2, H-1051, tel. 361/1383–000, fax 361/1188–659. 350 rooms, 24 suites. Facilities: 4 restaurants, bar, conference facilities, hairdresser, beauty salon, indoor swimming pool, health club, sauna, solarium, ballroom, private underground parking on site, valet services, travel arrangements, car hire, airport transfer service. Regency Club on 7th and 8th floors. AE, DC, MC, V.*

Budapest Hilton. Built in 1977 around a 13th-century monastery, adjacent to the Matthias Coronation Church and overlooking the Danube from the choicest site on Castle Hill, this perfectly integrated architectural wonder is a thrilling place. Guests stay in ample Hilton Contemporary rooms with double-sink bathrooms. Every room has a remarkable view; Danube vistas cost more. Much of Budapest's international business seems to be conducted in the lobby bar. You can gamble in the casino on the top floor, and the ground-level, Kalocsa dining room boasts some of Budapest's best folkloric decor, authentic Gypsy music, and cabbage strudel. For swimming and sauna, there is a free shuttle bus to the Thermal Hotel on Margaret Island, but it doesn't operate on weekends. Children, regardless of age, get free accommodation when sharing a room with their parents. Breakfast is not included in the room rate—a dubious distinction in Budapest; many guests are surprised, upon leaving an otherwise excellent morning feast, to be hit with a bill. *I, Hess András tér 1–3, H-1014, tel. 361/1751–000; in U.S., 800/445–8667; in Canada, 416/362–3771 or 800/268–9275; fax 361/1560–285. 323 rooms, 28 suites. Facilities: 2 restaurants, café, 2 bars; casino; hairdresser, cosmetic salon, garage, gift shops, flower shop, boutiques, antiques shop, IBUSZ and MALEV travel agency. AE, DC, MC, V.*

★ **Duna InterContinental.** The first of Budapest's big chain hotels opened its doors on December 31, 1969—and you can tell when it was built. It's a square, boxy bunker guarding the Danube on the Pest side between the Elizabeth and Chain bridges. But once you're past the inhospitable dark-wood lobby where you feel pressured to order a drink if you sit down, it's a different story. The staff is welcoming, the recreational facilities are the best downtown (including a squash court and a terrace for sunbathing), and every cozy, inviting, contemporary room has a balcony with a Danube view. Rooms are also equipped with special shaving plugs for 110-volt razors. The InterCont and its cousin next door, the Forum, were the city's first to have Cable News Network in English. The rooftop Bellevue Supper Club offers gourmet Hungarian and international cuisine to rival the spectacular view across the Danube to Castle Hill. There is no separate charge for children under 14 staying in their parents' room. *V, Apáczai Csere János utca 4, Box 100, H-1364, tel. 361/1175–122 or 361/1184–647; in U.S., 800/327–0200; in Canada, 800/268–3785; fax 361/1184–973. 340 rooms, 53 suites. Facilities: 3 restaurants, snack bar, 2 bars; business center, conference room; fitness center, squash court, IBUSZ desk, beauty salon, florist, art gallery, antiques shop, jewelry shop; parking. AE, DC, MC, V.*

★ **Forum.** In 1985, when the four-year-old Forum was named American Express Hotel of the Year in Europe and the Middle East, it was noted that the nearly two-to-one ratio of staff to rooms had much to do with its success. This is felt from the moment you enter the brightly lighted lobby; whether you need a message hand-delivered across town or a button sewn, the staff is always ready—though never fawning. The recently remodeled rooms, 60% of which have Danube views, are done in shades of red and cream, with welcoming upholstered furniture. On each of the Forum's eight floors is a small conference room that can be rented by the day or half day. In addition to the usual recreational amenities, the well-equipped Leisure Center offers a treadmill as well as manicure and pedicure services. The sepia-toned Silhouette Restaurant and Viennese Coffeehouse, popular with Hungarians as well as guests, have very good food. In Budapest, at least, Forum is no longer the budget stepchild of the InterContinental chain. There is no charge for children under 14 staying in their parents' room; a single-room rate is charged if two children share a connecting room. *V, Apáczai Csere János utca 12–14, Box 231, H-1368, tel. 361/1178–088 or 361/1177–730; in U.S., 800/327–0200; in Canada, 800/268–3785; fax 361/1179–808. 408 rooms, 16 suites. AE, DC, MC, V.*

Expensive

Aquincum. This classy, glassy spa hotel opened in May 1991. One of its three atriums lets the sun shine in on a long, sloping swimming pool heated to 25C (77F), a thermal pool heated to 31C (88F), a thermal healing pool heated to the fever pitch of 39C (102F), and a Jacuzzi. The thermal waters are piped in from a well on Margaret Island, which the Danube-view rooms overlook. The waters are considered therapeutic for rheumatic and arthritic problems, gout, circulatory disturbances, chronic bronchitis, recuperation from injuries, and even old age! The hotel's medical department specializes in balneotherapy (healing with mineral baths) and physical and electrical therapy. Most of the patrons, however, are business people and tourists who just want a place to swim before or after sightseeing. The hotel's location—on the Buda side near the Árpád Bridge—seems a minus, but it's remarkably handy to public transport to everywhere in town (and right off the HÉV suburban railway to Szentendre). It boasts a cordial, even chummy, front desk staff, who greet guests by name, and extraordinarily solicitous room service. Guest rooms are comfortable notwithstanding the fact that the decor is modern to the point of being spartan. *III, Árpád fejedlem útja 94, H-1036, tel. 361/188–6360, fax 361/168–8872. 312 rooms, all with bath. No-smoking rooms and rooms for the handicapped. Facilities: 2 restaurants, 2 bars, café; sauna, fitness center; business center; drug store, travel agency, car rental; minibars and TVs in all rooms; parking. AE, DC, MC, V.*

★ **Béke Radisson.** In 1975 it was a family-oriented inn where a room cost less than $6 a night; a decade later the well-situated Béke (on a main boulevard near the West Railroad Station) underwent a lavish overhaul. Today it is a luxury hotel with a glittering turn-of-the-century facade, a liveried doorman, a lobby lined with mosaics and statuary, and bellmen bowing before the grand staircase. Popular with Italians and Americans, this hotel has all the business amenities plus the efficient services of a helpful staff. Rooms resemble solidly modern living rooms; the dark furniture includes a round table that makes a good workspace. The breakfast buffet in the Shakespeare Room upstages a voluptuous *Twelfth Night* mural by offering the usual choices, all fresh and flavorful, plus creamy layer cakes and spicy stews that would make Sir Toby belch. At night, feast on the spectacle at the Orfeum night club. *VI, Teréz krt. 97, H-1067, tel. 361/1323–300, fax 361/1533–380. 238 rooms, 8 suites. Facilities: 2 restaurants, café, 2 bars, nightclub; business center, conference rooms; gift shops, travel agency; parking. AE, DC, MC, V.*

Buda Penta. Hard by the Déli (South) Railroad Station, and therefore convenient for jaunts to Vienna and most of Hungary, this is surely the least Hungarian-looking hotel in Buda, its orange exterior recalling Howard Johnson's. The Capri Pizzeria Pub (with Austrian draft beer) and Krisztina Espresso café leading in to the bustling lobby suggest Coney Island. The Airport modern rooms are small and orange, and ceilings are low everywhere—but so are the prices. With its Horoszkop Night

Club, Budapest's most popular disco, the Penta is a good place to stay if you want to feel like part of the capital's lively cosmopolitan scene. *I, Krisztina krt. 41–43, H-1013, tel. 361/1566–333; in U.S., 212/239–8810, 213/622–2753, or 800/225–3456; in Canada, 800/634–3421; fax 361/1556–964. 391 rooms, 8 suites. Facilities: restaurant, bar, café, sauna, swimming pool; business center. AE, DC, MC, V.*

Flamenco. Opened in 1989 next to a park with a lake in the Buda foothills, and convenient to downtown Pest via two nearby bridges, this Spanish-style hotel is a welcome addition to the ranks of luxury on the Buda side of the river. The vanilla-slab exterior and glitzy, spotlighted, low-ceiling lobby have no national character; but the rooms, decorated in a not very restful red and black, feel Spanish. So do the food and drink in the hotel's wine cellar, La Bodega, which Spaniards find spicier than those in Spain. The Flamenco is equipped with all the amenities for work and play (including access to a nearby tennis center), and the staff couldn't be nicer. Despite its garish decor, it can be one of the quietest, least bustling—in fact, almost residential—hotels in Budapest, when it isn't booked up with groups. *A HUSA Internacional hotel. XI, Tas vezér út 7, H-1113, tel. 361/1612–250 or 361/1669–619, fax 361/1658–007. 336 rooms, 12 suites. AE, DC, MC, V.*

★ **Gellért.** This most Hungarian of grand hotels lost a little of its lobby to a recent streamlining, but the double-deck rotunda still leaves you to expect a string orchestra, concealed behind massive marble pillars, playing "The Emperor Waltz." Indeed, the Jugendstil (Art Nouveau) Gellért (built in 1918, the year the Austro-Hungarian empire ended) is favored by Otto von Habsburg, son of the last emperor, and by that other deposed monarch, Richard Nixon. Rooms have early 20th-century furnishings, including some Jugendstil pieces, along with views across the Danube or up Gellért Hill. Rooms and amenities are up-to-date, and the coffee shop is among the city's best; but the pièce de résistance is the monumental thermal baths, including an outdoor pool with a wave machine. Admission to the spa is free to hotel guests (medical treatments cost extra); corridors lead directly to the baths from the second, third, and fourth floors. *XI, Gellért tér 1, H-1114, tel. 361/1852–200, fax 361/16–631. 221 rooms, 14 suites. Facilities: restaurant, café, thermal baths. AE, DC, MC, V.*

Grand Hotel Hungaria. Budapest's largest hotel, rebuilt in 1985 on the site of the old Hotel Imperial, stands on a busy boulevard just across an impossible traffic circle from the handsome Keleti (East) Station, where the Orient Express stops every day. Triple windows keep noise out of the large, homey rooms, with their upholstered chairs and orange-checked rugs; the best views are from the eighth floor facing the railroad terminal. The hotel is well equipped, and its staff is efficient, friendly, and at times amusing: the serious-looking fur-collared doorman could be patrolling what used to be the Iron Curtain instead of a revolving door. The lobby, on the other hand, could be that of any medium-size metropolitan hotel, except for the Lady Drink Bar at the end, which seems to be staffed and patronized exclusively by men. The coffee shop is a good early-morning rendezvous. The mattresses are hard on one side, soft on the other; chambermaids will flip them to your preference. *VII, Rákóczi út 90, H-1074, tel. 361/1229–050, fax 361/1228–029. 500 rooms, 28 suites. Facilities: restaurant, 2 bars, café. AE, DC, MC, V.*

★ **Helia.** Postcommunist Hungary's first privately built major hotel (financed with Hungarian, Finnish, and a little U.S. capital) opened in late 1990. The staff is friendly and helpful, and most of the comfortable rooms have Danube views. The reasonably priced restaurant open from morning to midnight, has an excellent hot and cold buffet, as well as an intimate French dining room. Best of all is Budapest's most enjoyable hotel swimming complex: sun terrace, hot thermal pool, two Jacuzzis, sauna, Turkish baths, and fitness center—all included in the room price. Located about 15 minutes by bus and ten minutes by metro from downtown, the Helia is the perfect place to combine a little rest and relaxation with sightseeing. *XIII, Karpát utca 62–64, H-1133, tel. 361/1298–650, 361/1495–170, 800/223–5652 in U.S. and Canada, fax 361/1201–429. 262 rooms, 4 suites with sauna, and 4 suites with bar. Facilities: restaurant, fitness center. AE, DC, MC, V.*

Novotel. This member of the French motor-inn chain is on the rim of a large park near the highways to Vienna and Lake Balaton. Connected to the Budapest Convention Center, it is favored by musicians as well as by convention delegates. Though the rooms are ordinary, with tiny bathrooms, soft mattresses, and a motel-generic decor, the amenities are more than ample: closed-circuit TV news in English, French, and German; a complete business center; outdoor tennis courts; a hydrotherapy program; an outdoor music pavilion; a duty-free shop that's strong on clothing and leather goods; and, famous around town, the Bowling Brasserie, featuring "fried meats, draft beer," and a bowling alley that turns into a hip disco on Thursday nights. This is a more rewarding chain-hotel environment than the Buda Penta. No charge is made for children under 16 staying in their parents' room. *XII, Alkotás út 63–67, Box 233, H-1444, tel. 361/1869–588; for reservations, 361/1669–031; in U.S., 213/277–6915; fax 361/1665–636. 317 rooms, 7 suites. Facilities: restaurant, bar, disco, tennis courts, fitness center; business center; parking. AE, DC, MC, V.*

Ramada Grand Hotel. On Margaret Island National Park, in the Danube between Buda and Pest, stands the world's stateliest Ramada, popular with movie stars and upscale tourists. The Grand Hotel Margitsziget, built in 1873 and long in disrepair, reopened in 1987 as a Ramada Inn. Room rates may have been raised, but the high ceilings haven't been lowered. Nor have the old-fashioned room trimmings—down comforters, ornate chandeliers, Old World furniture—been lost in the streamlining. Graham Greene always took the same suite that he had before World War II, and the U.S. Embassy likes to send visitors here. A heated tunnel connects the Ramada Grand to the Thermal hotel (*see below*) next door, where the pools, sauna, and mineral waters gurgle; Ramada guests are admitted free. They are also given preferred access to Hungary's first golf course, in Kisoroszi, 35 kilometers (22 miles) north of the city. *XIII, Margitsziget, H-1138, tel. 361/1111–000; for hotel guests, 361/1321–100; for reservations, 361/1317–769; in U.S., 800/228–9898; in Canada, 416/485–2610, 800/268–8930, or 800/268–8998; fax 361/1533–029. 153 rooms, 10 suites. Facilities: restaurant, fitness center. AE, DC, MC, V.*

Thermal. What the Prater is to Vienna, Margaret Island is to Budapest: an easily accessible sylvan setting for urban recreation. A bunker of concrete and glass, built in 1979, the Thermal does nothing to enhance the island's beauty, but it is a serious spa. The spacious accommodations look like luxurious hospital rooms, and they all have balconies and good views. Amusements include a casino and a nightclub—the Havana—with live Cuban music. The relaxing baths are included in the room price, as are a "drinking cure" (nonalcoholic sparkling water) and a dental exam. Hungary, with its well-trained dentists and porcelain craftspeople, is a mecca for cap and denture shoppers. The bargain packages include physicians' exams and treatments, particularly for muscular and rheumatic conditions, and still allow time for sightseeing. *XIII, Margitsziget, H-1138, tel. 361/1111–000, fax 361/1533–029. AE, DC, MC, V.*

Moderate

Astoria. At a busy intersection in downtown Pest stands a revitalized turn-of-the-century hotel that remains an oasis of quiet and serenity in hectic surroundings. In the green-and-golden, brown-wood and marble lobby, an unflappable clerk presides over the front desk. A brass bell summons staff members who are always—albeit unobtrusively—on hand. Rooms are genteel, spacious, and comfortable, furnished rather like grandma's sitting room, in slightly Victorian style with an occasional antique. Though the hotel lacks business and fitness centers, a sauna, or a swimming pool, it makes up for it with first-rate personal service and Old World charm—as well as moderate prices. This is one of the few hotels in Budapest where you can have clothing washed and pressed on a weekend. *V, Kossuth Lajos utca 19–21, H-1052, tel. 361/1173–411, fax 361/1186–798. 130 rooms, most convertible to suites. Facilities: restaurant, 2 bars, coffee shop, night club; IBUSZ desk, conference room. AE, DC, MC, V.*

Erzsébet. This well-known hotel with a long tradition of good service was torn down and rebuilt between 1978 and 1985. Located in the center of the Inner City, it boasts a popular beer cellar (János Pince) among its attractions. *V, Károly Mihály utca 11–15, tel. 361/1382–111, fax 361/1189–237. 123 rooms, mostly doubles with shower. Facilities: restaurant, bar, snack bar, beer hall; IBUSZ desk. AE, DC, MC, V.*

Nemzeti. Another hotel that reflects the grand mood of the turn of the century, Nemzeti was completely restored in 1987 and offers all the modern comforts. It's cozy, with a central location in Pest. *VIII, József krt. 4, tel. 361/1339–160, fax 361/1140–019. 76 rooms, mostly doubles with bath. Facilities: restaurant, brasserie. AE, DC, MC, V.*

Panorama Hotels-Bungalows (Vörös Csillag). Perched 310 meters (1,017 feet) above the Danube near the upper terminus of the cogwheel railway, Vörös Csillag resembles a hunting lodge. Unless you have vertigo, you will admire the view of the entire city from the terrace. *XII, Rege út 21, tel. 361/1750–522, fax 361/1750–412. 40 rooms with bath, 54 self-catering bungalows. Facilities: restaurant, bar terrace, pool, sauna. AE, DC, MC, V.*

Taverna. This 12-story, Austrian-built hotel is located in the heart of Pest's main shopping pedestrian zone, a few steps from the Danube and directly across Váci utca from International Trade Center 2; it was built around the same time (1985) and has a similar glass-needle style. The Taverna has an adequate range of facilities, and its cheerful, obliging staff makes Budapest less intimidating (and a good value) for the business traveler. Rooms are oases of impersonal serenity, with some Art

Nouveau furnishings, but if you're looking to enjoy the city's street life, it's right there in the 24-hour fast-food cafeteria and bowling alley/beer bar. *V, Váci utca 20, H-1052, tel. 361/138–5822, fax 361/1187–188. 196 rooms, 28 suites. Facilities: 2 restaurants, brasserie, 2 bars; sauna, solarium, massage. AE, DC, MC, V.*

Inexpensive

Citadella. Comparatively basic, with four beds in some rooms and showers down the hall, the Citadella is nevertheless very popular, particularly with young people, who enjoy the lively communal atmosphere and the location—right inside the fortress. *XI, Gellérthegy, tel. 361/1665–794. 40 rooms, none with bath. Facilities: restaurant, beer hall, nightclub. No credit cards.*

Wien. The Wien is located in the southwestern outskirts of the city, near the junction of the highways to Vienna and Balaton, making it popular and convenient for drivers. *XI, Budaörsi út 88, tel. 361/1665–400. 110 rooms, most with bath. Facilities: restaurant, café, gas station, car repairs. AE, DC, MC, V.*

The Arts and Nightlife

The Arts

Budapest's two major opera citadels, the **Hungarian State Opera House** and the **Erkel Theater**, present an international repertoire of classical and modern works as well as such Hungarian favorites as Kodaly's *Hary Janos*. The **Operetta Theater** features not just Lehar and Kalman but also *My Fair Lady*, *Fiddler on the Roof*, and a *Singing in the Rain* that Broadway director Harold Prince calls the best stage production he's ever seen. Four musical theaters—**Madach, Jozsef Attila, Vigszinhaz,** and **Pesti**—offer spectacles such as *Cats* and *Les Misérables* in Hungarian. There are also three major concert halls—the **Old** and **New Academy of Music** and the **Budapest Convention Center**—and a center for performances (Buda Concert Hall) by Hungarian folk dance ensembles. Most movies are shown in their original language.

Hotels and tourist offices will provide you with a copy of the monthly publication *Programme*, which contains details of all cultural events.

Ticket Offices   Theater and opera tickets are sold at the **Central Theater Booking Office** (VI, Andrassy útja 18, tel. 361/1120–000). For concert tickets, try **ORI** (V, Vörösmarty tér 1, tel. 361/1176–222). Prices are dirt-cheap, so markups of even 30% shouldn't dent your wallet if you book through your hotel. Other outlets for tickets are **Music Mix Ticket Service** (V, Barczy I. utca 1–3, tel. 361/1382–237 or 361/1171–385) and **Tourinform** (V, Suto utca 2, tel. 361/1188–718). Try also the offices at II, Moszkva tér 3 (tel. 361/1359–136) and VI, Andrassy út 18 (tel. 361/1120–000).

Music   **Academy of Music,** VI, Liszt Ferenc tér 8, tel. 361/1414–788; ticket office, tel. 361/1420–179.

Buda Concert Hall (folk dance), I, Corvin tér 8, tel. 361/1354–354.

Budai Vigadó (concert hall), I, Corvin tér 8, tel. 361/2015–928.

Budapest Convention Center (concerts and shows), XII, Jagello út 1–3, tel. 361/1869–588.

Erkel Theater (opera), VIII, Koztarsasag tér 30, tel. 361/1330–108; ticket office, tel. 361/1330–540.

Hungarian State Opera House, VI, Andrassy útja 22, tel. 361/1312–550; ticket office, tel. 361/1530–170.

Old Academy of Music, VI, Vörösmarty utca 35, tel. 361/1229–804.

Operetta Theater, VI, Nagymezo utca 17, tel. 361/1126–470; ticket office, tel. 361/1320–535.

Pesti Vigadó (concert hall), V, Vigadó tér 1, tel. 361/1189–903.

Theater **Arany Janos Színház**, VI, Paulay Ede utca 35, tel. 361/1415–626.

Jozsef Attila Theater, VII, Váci utca 63, tel. 361/1208–239; ticket office, tel. 361/1409–428.

Madach Theater, VII, Lenin körút 31–33, tel. 361/1220–677; ticket office, tel. 361/1222–015.

Merlin Színház, V, Gerloczy utca 4, tel. 361/1179–338.

Pesti Theater, V, Váci utca 9, tel. 361/1185–255; ticket office, tel. 361/1185–547.

Varszínház (Castle Theater), I, Színház utca 1–3, tel. 361/1758–649.

Vigszínház (Comedy Theater), XIII, Szent Istvan körút 14, tel. 361/1111–650; ticket office, 361/1110–430.

Galleries **Csok István Gallery**, V, Váci utca 25, tel. 361/1182–592.

Csontvary Gallery, V, Vörösmarty tér 1, tel. 361/1184–594.

Derkovits Gallery, VII, Teréz körút 9, tel. 361/1420–754.

Koszta Gallery, XI, Bartok Bela út 34. I. 2nd floor, tel. 361/1620–422.

Roczkov Gallery, VI, Andrássy utja 1, tel. 361/1426–834.

Nightlife

Bars and Lounges For quiet conversation, there are *drink-bárs* in most hotels and all over town, but beware of the inflated prices. Admission starts at 150 Ft.; drinks cost from 200 Ft. to 500 Ft. Coffeehouses are preferable for unescorted women.

Les Amis is a popular late-night eatery that offers some interesting curried dishes. *II, Rómer Flóris utca 12.*

Casanova offers music and dancing in an attractive building a few yards from the riverbank on the Buda side. *I, Batthyany tér 4, tel. 361/1338–320. Open 10 PM–4 AM.*

Duna-bar Boat sails up and down the river with dancing and disco music on board. *Board at Quay 3, opposite the Forum Hotel, on the Pest side. Tel. 361/1170–803. Open 10 PM–3 AM.*

Fregatt, an English-Irish pub popular with young expatriate Americans and Brits, features live music on the weekends. *V, Molnar utca 26.*

Nirvana Bar seems to be a leftover from a B-movie set. *V, Szent István körút 13.*

Piaf is popular but noisy and charges a modest entrance fee. *VI, Nagymezo utca 20.*

Pierrot is an elegant café in the Castle District and has live piano music and good cocktails. *I, Fortuna utca 14, tel. 361/1756–971. Open 5 PM–1 AM. No credit cards.*

Cabarets   **Horoszkop,** in the Buda-Penta Hotel, is the favorite among the younger set. Floor shows begin at 11 PM. *I, Krisztina körút 41–43, tel. 361/1566–333. Open 10 PM–4 AM.*

Maxim's, in the Hotel Emke, currently offers three variety shows daily plus a "Crazy Cabaret" show. *VII, Akácfa utca 3, tel. 361/1420–145. Open 8 PM–3 AM.*

Moulin Rouge, named after the Parisian original, is the place to go for a Vegas-style night out. The glitz comes with a higher price tag, however, and advance reservations are required. *VI, Nagymezo utca 17, tel. 361/1124–492). Performances at 9:30, 10, and midnight.*

Fortuna, opposite the Matthias Church on Castle Hill, is one of the city's most elegant night spots. It is located in the hall of a 14th-century building. The program starts at 12:30 AM. *I, Hess András tér, tel. 361/1557–451. Open 10 PM–4 AM.*

Discos   The university colleges organize the best discos in town. Try the **ELTE Club** (Eötvös Loránd) in the Inner City, on the corner of Károlyi Mihály utca and Irányi utca. Admission and the price of drinks are reasonable. Bring some student I.D.

3

The Danube Bend

Introduction

About 40 kilometers (25 miles) north of Budapest, the Danube abandons its eastward course and turns abruptly south toward the capital, cutting through the Börzsöny and Visegrád hills. This area is called the Danube Bend and includes the Baroque town of Szentendre, the hilltop castle ruins and town of Visegrád, and the cathedral town of Esztergom. The attractive combination of hillside and river should dispel any notion that Hungary is one vast, boring plain.

This is the most scenically varied part of Hungary. There is a whole chain of riverside spas and beaches, bare volcanic mountains, and limestone hills. Here, in the heartland, are the traces of the country's history—the remains of the Roman Empire's frontiers, the battlefields of the Middle Ages, and the relics of the Hungarian Renaissance.

The west bank of the Danube is the more interesting side, with three charming and picturesque towns—Szentendre, Visegrád, and Esztergom—all of which richly repay a visit. The district can be covered by car in one day, the total round-trip being no more than 112 kilometers (70 miles), although this would allow only a cursory look at the many places of interest. Two days, with a night at either Visegrád or Esztergom (both of which have good hotels), would suffice for a more thorough and leisurely look at this delightful part of Hungary. Vác is the only larger town on the east bank of any real interest. There are numerous ferries across the Danube, but no bridges, so that it's possible to combine a visit to both sides of the Danube on the same excursion. (There are ferry services between Visegrád and Nagymaros; Basaharc and Szob; Szentendre Island and Vác.)

Work had started in the mid-1980s on a hydro-electric dam near Nagymaros, across from Visegrád. The project was proposed by Austria and Czechoslovakia and reluctantly agreed to by Hungary, but protests from the Blues (Hungary's equivalent of Germany's Greens), coupled with rapid democratization, seem to have aborted the project and rescued a region of great natural beauty.

Essential Information

Important Addresses and Numbers

Tourist Information	**Esztergom** (IBUSZ Office, Széchenyi tér, tel. 1/484) **Szentendre** (Dunatours, Bacsó part 6, on the quay, tel. 26/11–311) **Vác** (IBUSZ, Széchenyi utca) **Visegrád** (Dunatours, Fő utca 3/A, tel. 26/28–330)
Emergencies	**Police:** tel. 07; **ambulance:** tel. 04; **fire;** tel. 05.
Late-night Pharmacies	In Szentendre, the pharmacy at Liget utca 5 (tel. 26/10–487) has late hours.
Travel Agencies	In Budapest, the main office of **Dunatours** can supply information about the Danube Bend (Bajcsy Zsilinszky út 17, tel. 361/111–5015 or 361/131–4533).

Esztergom: IBUSZ, Széchenyi tér, tel. 33/12–552.

Szentendre: **Dunatours,** Bacsó part 6, on the quay, tel. 26/11–311; **IBUSZ,** Bogdanyi utca 11, tel. 26/10–315.

Getting Around

If you have enough time, you can travel by boat from Budapest, a leisurely and pleasant journey, especially in summer and spring. The boats for Esztergom leave from the main Pest dock near Vigadó tér. On summer Sundays and public holidays a hydrofoil service brings Visegrád within an hour and Esztergom within two hours of Budapest. Timetables are on display at the dock (tel. 1181–223), in major hotels, and at most travel agencies in Budapest. Trains run frequently to Szentendre from Batthyány tér in Buda. By car via Szentendre-Visegrád, follow Highway 11, which more or less hugs the Buda bank of the Danube. A daylong coach tour is run by IBUSZ in the high season on Tuesday and Friday, visiting Szentendre, Visegrád, and Esztergom. It includes lunch and wine-tasting, costs around $40, and is strongly recommended. For a special steam train on weekends in the summer, contact MAV (Hungarian National Railways), or IBUSZ.

To reach Vác, go by boat from Budapest (Vigadó tér dock), by bus or train from the Nyugati (West) Station, or by car via Highway 2.

Guided Tours

IBUSZ organizes day trips from Budapest along the Danube from May through October, costing about 2,500 Ft. with lunch. Boat trips run on Wednesday and Saturday; buses go on Tuesday, Friday, and Saturday. There is also a special bus trip to Szentendre on Thursday.

Exploring the Danube Bend

Numbers in the margin correspond to points of interest on the Danube Bend map.

This tour moves northward along the west bank of the Danube, starting in Budapest in the district of Óbuda (for more information about Óbuda, *see* Tour 4 in Chapter 2). Szentendrei út, or Highway 11, is the main road leading to the Danube Bend; it begins at Flórian tér in Óbuda and leads first to the reconstructed remains of **Aquincum,** a Roman settlement dating from the 1st century AD and the capital of the Roman province of Pannonia. Before leaving the center of Óbuda, however, it's worth making a short detour to see the **Hercules Villa.** Just a few blocks west of Szentendrei út on Meggyfa utca, this fine 3rd-century Roman dwelling takes its name from the myth depicted on its beautiful mosaic floor. The ruin was unearthed between 1958 and 1967. *Meggyfa utca 19–21. tel. 1804–655. Admission: 10 Ft. Open May–Nov., Tues.–Sun. 10–6.*

Careful excavations at Aquincum have unearthed a varied selection of artifacts and mosaics, giving a tantalizing inkling of what life was like in the provinces of the Roman Empire. A gymnasium and a central heating system have been unearthed,

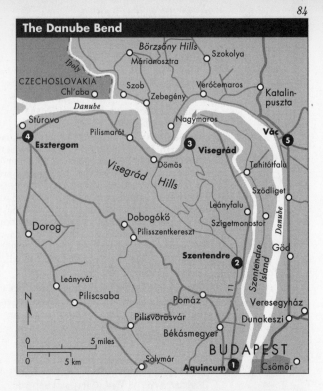

The Danube Bend

along with the ruins of two baths and a shrine to Mithras, the Persian god of light, truth, and the sun. Aquincum's aqueduct, which brought water from the Buda Hills and Danube springs, has been carefully reconstructed and may be viewed from Szentendrei út. The most notable buildings at the site are the basilica, the forum, and the public baths.

The **Aquincum Museum** displays the dig's most notable finds: ceramics signed by the city's best-known potter, Ressatus of Aquincum; a red-marble sarcophagus showing a triton and flying Eros on one side and, on the other side, Telesphorus, the angel of death, depicted as a hooded dwarf; and jewelry from a Roman lady's tomb. One of the most intriguing items in the collection is the water organ, the only Roman organ that has been preserved and can still be played. Although its wood parts have decayed, all 52 of its bronze pipes were found. Its bellows work by hydraulic pressure; atmospheric pressure is regulated by weights. *Szentendrei út 139, tel. 361/168–8241. Admission: 10 Ft. adults, 5 Ft. children and students. Open May–Nov., Tues.–Sun. 10–6.*

Just beyond Aquincum is the **Római fürdő** (Roman Bath), one of Budapest's two main campsites and one of the city's most enjoyable open-air bathing areas. *Tel. 361/180–4650. Open May–Nov., Tues.–Sun. 10–6.*

Rising above Óbuda and Aquincum are the thickly wooded **Buda Hills**, the city's "green lung" and biggest playground, full of hikers and picnickers in summer and skiers and sledders in winter. The area is easily accessible by public transport. A favorite way to make the ascent is to ride the cogwheel railway that starts opposite the Hotel Budapest and climbs to **Széchenyi Hill.** On Szilágyi Erzsébet fasor, the tree-lined boulevard leading to the Hotel Budapest, stands a new bronze **statue of Raoul Wallenberg,** the Swedish diplomat who saved some 100,000 Hungarian Jews during World War II and then disappeared in early 1945 near Debrecen, while in the custody of the advancing Red Army.

2 **Szentendre** (Saint Andrew), some 20 kilometers (12 miles) to the north, is the pearl of the Danube Bend: a romantic town of about 17,000 inhabitants. Nowadays a flourishing artists' colony with a lively Mediterranean atmosphere, Szentendre was first settled by Serbs and Greeks fleeing the advancing Turks in the 14th and 17th centuries. They built houses and churches in their own style—rich in reds and blues seldom seen elsewhere in Hungary. The local cuisine, too, has a Mediterranean flavor.

To savor Szentendre before you start sightseeing, stroll along the flower-lined **Danube Promenade** between the Boat Landing and Görög utca, ducking into any and every little cobblestoned side street that appeals to you. Baroque houses with shingled roofs (often with an arched eye-of-God upstairs window) and shingled walls will enchant your eye and pique your curiosity. Once the side streets cross Bogdányi utca, which parallels the riverfront, they rise into the hills above the town—which are worth exploring, too.

Görög utca (Greek Street) begins with a Greek restaurant, Görög Kancsó (The Grecian Urn), at No. 1 (*see* Dining, *below*) and ends inevitably at the so-called **Greek Church,** which is actually a Serbian Orthodox church that takes its name from the Greek inscription on a red marble gravestone set in its wall. This elegant edifice was built between 1752 and 1754 by a Rococo master, Andreas Mayerhoffer, on the site of a wooden church dating to the Great Serbian Migration (around 690); and its deed of foundation is written in Old Church Slavonic. Its greatest glory—a symmetrical floor-to-ceiling panoply of stunning icons—was painted between 1802 and 1804 by Mihailo Zivkovic, a Serbian painter from Buda.

Though you enter it on Görög utca, the Greek Church fronts on Fő tér (Main Square), the centerpiece of which is an ornate **Memorial Cross** erected by Serbs in gratitude for the town's being spared a plague. The cross has a crucifixion painted on it and stands atop a triangular pillar adorned with a dozen icon paintings. During the overlapping Szentendre Spring, Szentendre Summer, and Szentendre Days (these festivals of music, theater, and art covering most of the warm-weather season from late March to early September), you are likely to witness a Cimarosa or Mozart opera performed in the square by an ensemble from Budapest with full chamber orchestra. Every house on Fő (formerly Marx) tér is a designated landmark and three of them are open to the public: the **Ferenczy Museum** at No. 6 with paintings of Szentendre landscapes and statues and tapestries by a distinguished family of artists; the **Kmetty Museum** at no. 21 with works of Hungarian cubist painters, and the **Szentendre Képtát** (Municipal Gallery) at Nos. 2–5 with local contemporary art. *Admission to all 3 museums: 20 Ft. adults, 10 Ft. children. Open Tues.–Sun., 10–6.*

The roads uphill from Fő tér lead to at least two more churches: Atop **Vár-domb** (Castle Hill) is the town's oldest monument, the **Catholic Parish Church,** dating to the 13th century. After many reconstructions, its oldest visible part is a 15th-century sundial in the doorway, outside which is an arts-and-crafts market and, on weekends in summer, all-day entertainment. On the adjoining hill, also reached from Fő tér, stands the imposing red **Serbian Orthodox Cathedral,** built in the 1740's with a much more lavish but far less beautiful iconostasis than in the Greek Church below it. In a restful park in the religious complex is the **Cathedral Museum** with icons, altars, robes, 16th-century prayer books, and a 17th-century cross with a bullet hole through it. *Alkotmány utca 9, tel. 26/12–399. Admission: 30 Ft. adults, 15 Ft. children. Open Wed.–Sun. 10–4.*

Not far from Fő tér is another charming square, **Városház tér** (City Hall Square). What looks like a frontier trading post—consisting of a matching optical shop and Bank of Budapest branch—stares at the yellow Baroque **City Hall** while a gaily painted saint stands guard in a sentry niche at a corner of the square.

Szentendre has even more museums than churches, with the farthest-flung being the **Szabadtéri Néprajzi Múzeum** (Open-air Ethnographic Museum). Located 5 kilometers (3 miles) to the northwest, it is reachable by bus from the Szentendre terminus of the HÉV suburban railway. It is a re-creation of 18th- and 19th-century village life, with wooden houses with folk furniture, stables, and baking ovens; Reformed church, belfry, and graveyard; and a blacksmith shop and a mill powered by horses. *Szabadságforrás út, tel. 26/12304 . Admission: 25 Ft. Open Apr.–Oct., Tues.–Sun. 10–6.*

If you have only one museum to visit in Szentendre, don't miss the **Margit Kovács Museum,** the collected ceramics of a Budapest artist who died in 1977, leaving behind a wealth of richly textured work. Because you will be tempted to reach out and touch some of the people she has put before you, her museum limits admission to 15 persons at a time. Thus, it is wise to line up early or at lunch time, when tour groups are occupied elsewhere. *Vastagh György utca 1 (off Görög utca), tel. 26/10244. Admission: 25 Ft. Open Tues.–Sun. 10–4.*

❸ Continue north along the west bank of the Danube for 23 kilometers (14 miles)—past Leányfalu, a pleasant holiday resort with a tourist hotel and a campsite—to **Visegrád.** This was the seat of the Hungarian kings in the 14th century, when a citadel built here by the Angevin kings became the royal residence. If you only have a short time to visit Visegrád, spend it at the **Citadel,** at the top of the hill overlooking the village. Visegrád's chief attraction, the Citadel is in a better state of repair than the Royal Palace (*see below*) and offers better views of the Danube and the surrounding territory. *Admission: 16 Ft. adults, 4 Ft. children. Open daily 9–6.*

A century later, King Matthias Corvinus had a separate palace built on the banks of the Danube. Now the **Mátyás Király Múzeum,** its entrance is in the main street, Fő utca. It was razed by the Turks, and not until 1934 were the ruins excavated. Especially worth seeing is the red marble well built by a 15th-century Italian architect and decorated with the arms of

King Matthias. It is situated in a ceremonial courtyard, which has been restored in accordance with contemporary records. Above the courtyard rise the various halls; on the left you can still see a few fine original carvings, which give an idea of how magnificent the palace must have been. Don't fail to walk or drive up to the remains of the citadel, which provides a superb view. The nearby Nagy Villám Hill lookout tower offers spectacular views of the Danube Bend. *Fő utca 29, tel. 26/28026 or 26/28252. Admission: 10 Ft. adults, children free. Open May–Nov., Tues.–Sun. 9–5; Nov.–Apr., Tues.–Sun. 8–4.*

❹ **Esztergom,** 21 kilometers (13 miles) upriver, stands on the site of a Roman fortress. St. Stephen, the first Christian king of Hungary, was crowned here in the year 1000.

The **Esztergom Cathedral,** the largest in Hungary, stands on a hill overlooking the town; it is now the seat of the cardinal primate of Hungary. Its most interesting features are the **Bakócz chapel** (1506), named after a primate of Hungary who only narrowly missed becoming pope; and the sacristy, which contains a valuable collection of medieval ecclesiastical art. *Szent István tér. Admission free. Open June–Oct., daily 5:30–5; Nov.–May, daily 5:30–4.*

Below Cathedral Hill lie the streets of **Víziváros** (Watertown), lined with Baroque buildings. The **Keresztény Muzeum** (Museum of Christian Art) is situated in the Primate's Palace. It is the finest art gallery in Hungary, with a large collection of early Hungarian and Italian paintings. The Italian collection of 14th- and 15th-century works is unusually large for a museum outside Italy. A special treasure is the so-called *Coffin of Our Lord* from Garamszentbenedek, now in Czechoslovakia; the wooden statues of the Apostles and of the Roman soldiers guarding the coffin are masterpieces of Hungarian 15th-century sculpture. The building also houses the Primate's Archives, which contains 20,000 volumes, including several medieval codices. Permission to visit the Archives must be obtained in advance. When, in the 14th century, Buda became the political capital of Hungary, Esztergom remained—and still is—the ecclesiastical capital. *Primate's Palace, Berényi út 2. Admission: 15 Ft. Open Tues.–Sun. 10–6.*

To the north of the cathedral, on **Szent Tamás Hill,** is a small church dedicated to St. Thomas à Becket of Canterbury. From here you can look down on the town and see how the Danube temporarily divides, forming an island that locals use as a base for waterskiing and swimming.

At Esztergom, the Danube is now the frontier with Czechoslovakia. The bridge is no longer in existence, though parts of it can still be seen. A ferry now shuttles passengers across the border; at press time, only passengers with Hungarian or Czechoslovakian passports were permitted to use this crossing.

❺ The only town of importance on the east bank, **Vác,** is 34 kilometers (21 miles) from Budapest and can be reached either by road or rail. The town's two chief monuments are its Cathedral, built in 1763–77 by Archbishop Migazzi to the designs of the Italian architect Isidor Canevale; and a triumphal arch by the same architect erected to celebrate the visit of the Empress Maria Theresa.

Along the Danube north of Vác lie a string of pleasant summer resorts, nestling below the picturesque Börzsöny Hills and stretching as far as Szob, just east of the Slovak frontier.

Sports and Fitness

Szentendre   The waterfront and streets beyond Szentendre's main square are perfect for a bike ride—very wide and relatively calm and quiet; rentals are available from IBUSZ and Dunatours (*see* Tourist Information, *above*).

Take advantage of Szentendre's riverside location and head to the **Wiking Motor Yacht Club** (Ady Endre út 3, tel. 26/11–707), a short walk north along the Danube from the center of town. From May through October the yacht club offers expensive water-ski rentals (6,000 Ft. an hour), jet-ski rentals (7,200 Ft. an hour for 2 people; 6,000 Ft. for 1), canoe and kayak rentals (both 500 Ft. an hour). The rentals are available on the dock daily from 9–8. The club's main office is located on a ship (which also houses a good restaurant).

Pamáz, just 15 minutes away from Szentendre by HÉV, is known for its well-respected **riding school,** *Pomazi Lovásiskola.* Reasonably experienced riders can enjoy one-hour excursions (cost: 400 Ft.) through a 3-acre range near Kőhegy and Meseliahegy (Stone and Fabulous Hill), at the foot of the Pilis Mountain range. Schiffer Sándor, the owner of the school, takes good care of his team of 10 Hungarian half-bloods and gives riding lessons for 300 Ft. per half hour. Reservations are preferred; if you call the school after 4 PM you have a good chance of reaching someone who speaks English.

Visegrád   A well-marked **hiking trail** (with red signs) leads from the edge of Visegrad to Pilisszéntlaszlo: a wonderful journey among the oak and beech trees of the Visegrád Hills into the Pilis conservation region. Bears, bison, deer, and wild boar roam freely here; less menacing flora include fields of yellow blooming spring pheasant's eye and black pulsatilla.

Dining and Lodging

Dining

Category	Cost*
Very Expensive	over 1,200 Ft.
Expensive	1,000 Ft.–1,200 Ft.
Moderate	600 Ft.–1,000 Ft.
Inexpensive	under 600 Ft.

per person, including appetizer, entrée, and dessert and excluding drinks and 10%–15% service charge

Lodging

Category	Cost*
Very Expensive	7,000 Ft.–9,000 Ft.
Expensive	6,000 Ft.–7,000 Ft.

Moderate	3,500 Ft.–6,000 Ft.
Inexpensive	1,200 Ft.–3,500 Ft.

All prices for a standard double room, including breakfast and tax.

Esztergom
Dining

Kispipa. A lively and popular establishment, not far from the town center, the Kispipa is memorable for its good choice of wines. *Kossuth Lajos utca 19. No telephone. No reservations. No credit cards. Moderate.*

Alabárdos. This restaurant, attached to the panzió of the same name, comes highly recommended by locals. A pianist plays during dinner hour while customers eat by candlelight in carved-wood booths. The Hungarian meatballs are particularly tasty. *Bajcsy-Zsilinszky utca 49, tel. 33/12–640. No reservations. Dress: casual. No credit cards. Closed Mon. Inexpensive.*

Halászcsárda. Eating here also allows you to explore the small island formed by the branching of the Danube. Small, friendly, and informal, the Halászcsárda has a good selection of fish specialties. *Szabad Május sétány 14. No telephone. No reservations. No credit cards. Inexpensive.*

Lodging

Fürdő. This large hotel, near the center of town, has tennis courts and is attached to the local spa, which has an open-air swimming pool. *Bajcsy-Zsilinszky utca 14, tel. 33/10292. 85 rooms with bath. Facilities: restaurant, bar. No credit cards. Moderate.*

Vadvirág. A small guest house on the outskirts of town, Vadvirág offers simple accommodations, a restaurant, and tennis courts. *Bánomi üdülő, tel. 33/1174. 28 rooms, some with bath. No credit cards. Closed Oct.–Apr. Inexpensive.*

Szentendre
Dining
★

Viking. The restaurant of the Viking Motor Yacht Club is, appropriately, a boat moored on the Danube and featuring fish specialties. The atmosphere is irresistible with a one-man band singing along with his synthesizer at night; on some summer evenings, there is a show of Gypsy music, song, and dance. The "Viking Secret" appetizer is cold fogas, herring, and cockle salad with caviar and a stuffed egg. There is crayfish cream soup as well as Danube fish soup. A recommended hot appetizer is the Sailor's Stuffed Pancake of oven-baked caviar in a cheese sauce. Interesting main dishes on the English-language menu include "grilled catfish fillet tasted with garlic," "squid in beer cake," paprika catfish, and crayfish ragout in dill-cream sauce. There is also a salad bar. *Ady Endre út 3, tel. 26/11707. Reservations advised. Dress: informal. AE, DC, MC, V. Closed Nov.–Mar. Expensive.*

★

Aranysárkány. A little above the city on the way up to the Serbian Orthodox Cathedral, the Golden Dragon lies in wait with seven large tables, which you share with strangers on a busy night. The delicious food is prepared before your eyes in a turbulent open kitchen where dishes break and exuberance is rampant. All the activity is justified by the cold cherry soup with white wine and whipped cream or the hot Dragon Soup with quail eggs, meatballs, and vegetables. Try the grilled goose liver Oroszház-style wrapped in bacon and accompanied by a layered potato-and-cheese cake, broccoli, and a grilled tomato flying a basil-leaf flag. The "Dragon's Feast" is stuffed breast of young hen, and "lamb from the pasture" is prepared with red wine, garlic, and tarragon. The apricot pudding and cheese dumplings are also recommended. *Alkotmány utca 1/a, tel. 26/ 11670, telex 22–3333. Reservations advised. Dress: casual. No credit cards. Moderate.*

Béke. You won't find its name on this traditional restaurant in a 1750 Baroque house in the main square—just the word Privát in handsome gold letters. Fish and Hungarian specialties are better than ever, and the view of local comings and goings from its sidewalk café is unmatched. *Fő tér 19, tel. 26/11516. Reservations not necessary. Dress: casual. No credit cards. Moderate.*

Popeye. An *Eszpresszo-Snak Bar* from 9 AM to 8 PM, this place turns into a dance hall with go-go girls from 10 PM to 5 AM. *Bogdányi utca 13 (enter from Somogyi-Bacsó on the waterfront after 10 PM). Moderate.*

Régi Módi. This attractive upstairs restaurant is approached through a courtyard across from the Kovács Margit Múzeum. The bright decor, fine wines, and game specialties compensate for the slow service. *Futó utca 3, tel. 26/11–105. Reservations advised. No credit cards. Moderate.*

Görög Kancsó. The Grecian urn from which the inn takes its name is displayed and illuminated in a handsome interior room, but in summer most of the dining and socializing takes place in the garden restaurant on the bank of the Danube. Greek specialties and Hungarian pork livers are given equal care and flavor; the help is young and charming—and efficient, too. *Görög utca 1, no telephone. Reservations not necessary. Dress: casual. No credit cards. Inexpensive.*

Lodging **Bükkös Panzió.** West of Fő tér and across the bridge over Bükkös brook, this is one of the most conveniently located hotels in the village. Just five minutes from the HÉV and bus stations, it books up well in advance during July and August, so plan ahead. *Bükkös part 16, tel. 26/12–021. 16 rooms with bath. Facilities: restaurant, bar. No credit cards. Moderate.*

Coca-Cola Panzió. Removed just enough from busy motorway 11 to offer a sound night's sleep, this cozy and relatively modern panzió offers all the comforts of home, plus a grassy lawn, a picnic table, and a barbecue pit. You can even call home on the international red phone in the lobby. It's a five-minute walk from the town center and directly opposite the bus stop. *Dunakanyar krt. 50, tel. 26/10–410. 12 rooms with bath. Facilities: restaurant. No credit cards. Moderate.*

Danubius. On the highway near the Danube bank, north of town, this very ordinary hotel is considered the best in an area where most visitors are day excursionists on outings from Budapest, motorists just passing through the area, and campers. Rooms are small, bathrooms tiny; the staff is obliging. *Ady Endre út 28, H-2000, tel. 26/12489 or 26/12511, telex 22-4300. 48 rooms and 2 apartments, all with bath. Facilities: restaurant, tavern, bowling alley, barbecue. AE, DC, MC, V. Moderate.*

Fenyves. Atop a flight of stone steps, this rundown but striking villa is basically a bed-and-breakfast with luxury trappings— but one big drawback: no bath in any of the spacious, comfortable rooms. (There is plenty of plumbing down the halls.) *Ady Endre út 26, H-2000, tel. 26/11882. 9 rooms; no baths in rooms. Facilities: TV, refrigerator, and sink in rooms; outdoor pool, playground, sun terrace. No credit cards. Inexpensive.*

Hárgita Eldorádo Panzió. Named after the Hárgita Mountains in Transylvania, this newly remodeled panzió atop a grassy incline has all the makings of a Swiss chalet. Attic space has been converted into modernized rooms with television sets and sparkling tile showers. On a warm day, you can eat breakfast on the outside patio, accompanied by Donci, the caretaker's pet sheep. *Egressy út 22, tel. 26/11–928. 10 rooms with bath. Facilities: restaurant, kitchen for guest use. AE, MC, V. Moderate.*

Papszigeti Camping. On Szentendre Island in the Danube, this campsite also offers a good range of housing for the nonmotorized, non-tent-bearing traveler. *Papsziget, H-2000 Szentendre, tel. 26/10697, telex 22–4300. Camping places for 220 trailers and tents, 14 bungalows, and 5 rooms with bath; 10 motel rooms and 40-bed hostel. Facilities: beach, water sports. Closed mid-Oct.–Apr. Inexpensive.*

Visegrád
Dining

Diófa Kisvendéglő. Don't let the ugly dining room ward you away from this restaurant, which has a refreshing outdoor patio in back. The service is prompt and the dishes cheap. (Be warned, however, that slightly higher summer prices aren't marked on the winter menus; ask for prices before ordering.) The menu includes pork cutlets and a tasty vegetarian mushroom salad, but try the fried carp, a local specialty. *Fő út 48, tel. 26/28–131. No reservations. Dress: casual. No credit cards. Moderate.*

Fekete Holló. Popular with visitors and locals, the Black Raven restaurant has an elegant yet comfortable atmosphere. It's a great place for a full meal or just a beer. Try the Hungarian beef stew with potatoes, but save room for *palacsinta* (sweet pancakes with fruit or chocolate). *Rév út 15, tel. 26/28–158. No reservations. Dress: casual. No credit cards. Moderate.*

Sirály Restaurant. Right across from the ferry station, the Sirály (seagull) is one of Visegrad's more expensive restaurants and is justifiably well regarded for its cuisine. Skip the bland room indoors and head for a table on the outdoor patio, which has a great view of the Danube. In addition to rolled fillet of deer Visegrád style, there are five vegetarian dishes, including fried soyasteak with vegetables. On Friday and Saturday nights the place is transformed into a rocking disco. *Rév út 7, tel. 26/28–158. Reservations advised. Dress: casual but neat. No credit cards. Closed Nov.–early Mar. Moderate.*

Lodging

Silvanus. Located on a hill and offering spectacular views the Silvanus is recommended for motorists. There is a tennis court and linking trails in the forest for the more active. *Fekete-hegy, tel. 27/28–311. 79 rooms, most with bath. Facilities: restaurant, brasserie, terrace café. AE, DC, MC, V. Moderate.*

Hotel Eötvös. Just north of the town center, this hotel has freshly painted walls, new carpeting, and shiny, clean bathrooms. Breakfast is included in the price of a room. All guest rooms are minimally furnished doubles or triples. *Fő út 117, tel. 26/28–165. 33 rooms with bath. Facilities: restaurant. No credit cards. Inexpensive.*

Vár. Situated at the foot of a steep hill beside the Danube, this is a good choice for those whose priorities include scenery and the great outdoors. There are excellent water-sports facilities nearby, but the accommodations are very simple. *Fő utca 9–11, tel. 27/28–264. 15 double rooms, all with hot water but no bath. No credit cards. Inexpensive.*

4 Lake Balaton

Introduction

Lake Balaton, the largest lake in Central Europe, stretches 80 kilometers (50 miles) across Hungary. Just 90 kilometers (56 miles) to the southwest of Budapest, it is within easy reach of the capital by any means of transportation and is widely regarded as the most popular playground of this landlocked nation. On its hilly northern shore, ideal for growing grapes, is **Balatonfüred,** Hungary's oldest and most famous spa town. The national park on the **Tihany peninsula** is just to the south, and regular boat service links Tihany and Balatonfüred with Siófok on the southern shore. Although this shore is not as attractive as the northern one—being flatter and more crowded with resorts, cottages, and trade-union rest houses, its shallower, warmer waters make it a better choice for swimming than other locations.

A circular tour taking in Veszprém, Balatonfüred, and Tihany could be managed in a day. Two days, with a night in Tihany or Balatonfüred, would allow for detours to Herend and its porcelain factory, or to the castle at Nagyvázsony.

Essential Information

Important Addresses and Numbers

Tourist Information Two separate agencies provide information about the Balaton region: **Balatontourist** covers the northern shore, and **Siotour** disseminates information about the southern shore. Here are the addresses of the main Balatontourist offices:

Balatonfüred (Blaha Lujza utca 5, tel. 86/42–822 or 86/43–471)
Budapest (Üllői út 52/a, tel. 361/1336–982, fax 361/1339–929)
Nagyvázsony (Kinizsi vár, tel. 80/64–318)
Tihany (Kossuth utca 20, tel. 86/48–512 or 86/48–519)
Veszprém (Münnich F. tér 3, tel. 80/13–750, and Kossuth Lajos utca 21, tel. 80/29–630, fax 80/27–062)

Siotour has offices in the following cities:

Balatonföldvár (Hosök utja 9–11, tel. 84/40–099)
Budapest (Klauzal tér 2–3, tel. 361/1126–080)
Fonyód (Vasutallomas, tel. 84/61–214)
Siófok (Szabadsag ter 6, tel. 84/10–900)
Zamárdi (Petőfi út 1, tel. 84/31–072)

Emergencies Police: tel. 07; **ambulance:** tel. 04; **fire:** tel. 05.

Getting Around

By Car Road 71 runs along the northern shore; M7 covers the southern shore. Traffic can be heavy during summer weekends, and driving can be slow around the lake.

By Train Trains from Budapest serve all the resorts on the northern shore; a separate line links resorts on the southern shore. An express train from Budapest takes just over two hours to reach Siófok or Balatonfüred. Make sure to book tickets ahead of time.

By Bus Bus service links most resorts. Book ahead to avoid a long wait for a bus.

By Boat The slowest but most scenic way to travel is to use the ferries that link the major resorts. MAHART schedules are available from most of the tourist offices listed above.

Guided Tours

IBUSZ has several tours to Balaton from Budapest; inquire at the head office in Budapest, Petöfi tér 3, tel. 361/1185–707. Other tours more easily organized from hotels in the Balaton area include boat trips to vineyards, folk music evenings, and overnight trips to local inns.

Exploring Lake Balaton

Tour 1: The Northern Shore

Numbers in the margin correspond to points of interest on the Lake Balaton map.

❶ **Balatonfüred**, the lake's oldest and most internationally noted health resort, has every amenity. Above its beaches and promenade, the twisting streets of the **Old Town** climb hillsides thickly planted with vines. The hills protect the town from northerly winds. There is plenty of sunshine but also pleasant shade—ideal for a spa. Balatonfüred's 11 medicinal springs are said to have stimulating and beneficial effects on the heart and nerves. The climate and landscape also make this one of the best wine-growing districts in Hungary.

Great plane and poplar trees welcome you as you arrive at the busy boat-landing, where you can also park your car and start your stroll by ascending to the center of town in **Gyógy tér (Spa Square)**, where the bubbling waters from five volcanic springs rise beneath a slim, colonnaded pavilion. In the square's centerpiece, the neo-Classical **Well house** of the Kossuth Spring, you can sample the water, which has a pleasant, surprisingly cool taste. All of the buildings on the square are pillared like Greek temples. At No. 3 is the **Horváth House,** where the Szentgyörgyi–Horváth family arranged the first ball in 1825 in honor of their daughter Anna. It was there that she fell in love with Ernö Kiss, who became a general in the 1848–49 War of Independence and died a hero.

The Anna Balls, the nearest event that Lake Balaton has to a debutante cotillion, are now held every July in another colonnaded building on the square, the **Trade Unions' Sanatorium** (1802). Under its arcades is the **Balaton Pantheon:** aesthetically interesting tablets and reliefs honoring Hungarian and foreign notables who either worked for Lake Balaton or spread the word about it. Among them is the Czech author of *The Good Soldier Schweik*, Jaroslav Hašek, who also wrote tales of the Balaton. On the eastern side of the square is the **Cardiac Hospital**, where hundreds of patients from all over the world are treated. Here, too, Rabindranath Tagore, the Indian author and Nobel Prize winner, recovered from a heart attack in 1926. The tree that he planted to commemorate his stay still stands in a little grove at the bottom of steps leading from the square down to lakeside. Tagore also wrote a poem for the planting, which is memorialized beneath the tree on a strikingly animated bust of Tagore:

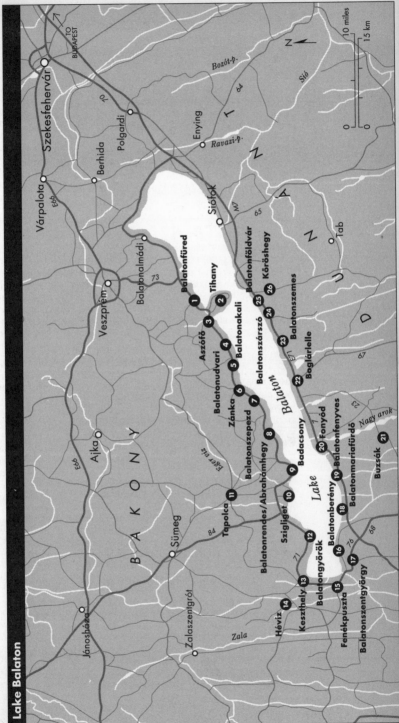

Lake Balaton

When I am no longer on earth, my tree,
Let the ever-renewed leaves of thy spring
Murmur to the wayfarer:
The poet did love while he lived.

In the same grove are trees honoring visits by another Nobel laureate, the Italian poet Salvatore Quasimodo, in 1961, and Indian Prime Minister Indira Gandhi, in 1972. An adjoining grove honors Soviet cosmonauts and their Hungarian partner-in-space, Bertalan Farkas. It opens onto the **Tagore sétány (Tagore Promenade)** nearly a kilometer (almost ½ mile) long and lined by trees, restaurants, and shops.

Time Out   A restful old-fashioned place where you can muse on the Tagore Promenade and the lake is the elegant **Balaton Restaurant** at Tagore sétány 5. Sip a drink and enjoy homemade pastries or plum dumplings to the accompaniment of cocktail music.

Back up at Gyógy tér, if you follow **Blaha Lujza utca,** you will happen upon such gems as the **Lujza Blaha House,** a neo-Classical villa built in 1867 that later became the summer house of this famous turn-of-the-century actress and singer; a **pharmacy** (1782); and the **Round Church (Kerek templom)** built in 1841–46. Behind the church is the summer house of the Hungarian author Mór Jókai, now a museum honoring his work. *Honvéd utca 1. Admission: 20 Ft. adults, 10 Ft. children. Open Feb.–Oct., Tues.–Sun. 10–6.*

Time Out   At Blaha Lujza utca 7 is a landmark built in 1795, the red plush **Kedves Café,** Lake Balaton's most popular and famous pastry shop. It is frequented in summer by actors and writers, who give periodic readings on the premises; there is also a Sunday morning puppet show for children. The Kedves also boasts a summer garden and a first-class restaurant.

Entered from the west of Balatonfüred (south off Highway 71) is the **Tihany Peninsula.** Joined to the mainland by a narrow neck and jutting 5 kilometers (3 miles) into the lake. Only 12 square kilometers (less than 5 square miles), the peninsula is not only a major tourist resort but perhaps the most historic part of the Balaton area. In 1952, the entire peninsula was declared a national park and, because of its geological rarities, it became Hungary's first nature-conservation zone. On it are over 110 geyser craters, remains of former hot springs, reminiscent of Yellowstone Park's, Iceland's, and Siberia's. As the peninsula broadens, you pass two lakes. The **Külső Tó (Outer Lake),** which dried up two centuries ago and was then used as pasture, has recently been refilled with water. The smooth **Belső Tó (Inner Lake),** 25 meters (82 feet) higher than Lake Balaton, is more impressive. Around it are barren yellowish-white rocks and volcanic cones rising against the sky. Standing atop any hill in the area, you can see water in every direction. While the hills surrounding the lake are known for their white wines, the peculiarities of this peninsula give rise to a notable Hungarian red, Tihany cabernet.

Between the Inner Lake and the eastern shore of the peninsula ❷ lies the village of **Tihany,** crowned by its **Abbey** with foundations laid by King Andras I in 1055. Only its Romanesque crypt, in which the king is buried, remains. (The Abbey's charter—containing some 100 Hungarian words in its Latin text make it the oldest written source of the Hungarian language—is kept in Pannonhalma.) Rebuilt in Baroque style between 1719 and 1784, the Abbey church towers above the village in feudal splendor. Its gilded silver high altar, abbot's throne, pulpit, organ case, choir parapet, and swirling crowd of saintly and angelic faces are all the work (between 1753 and 1765) of Sebestyén Stuhlhoff. A joiner from Augsburg, Stulhoff lived and worked in the monastery as a lay brother for 25 years after the death of his Hungarian sweetheart. Local tradition says that he immortalized her features in the angel kneeling on the right-hand side of the altar to the Virgin Mary. Pink angels float across the ceiling fresco; and the magnificent Baroque organ, adorned by stucco cherubs, can be heard on Tuesday and Wednesday evenings in summer.

In a Baroque house adjoining the Abbey is the Tihany **Historical Museum,** visited by more than 100,000 tourists annually. The best exhibits are in the basement lapidarium: relics from Roman colonization, including mosaic floors; a relief of David from the second or third century AD, and 1,200-year-old carved stones—all labeled in English as well as Hungarian. Three of the upstairs rooms were lived in for five days in 1921 by the last emperor of the dissolved Austro-Hungarian monarchy, Karl IV, in a futile foray to regain the throne of Hungary. Banished to Madeira, he died of pneumonia there a year later. The rooms are preserved with nostalgic relish for Franz Joseph's doomed successor and his empress, Zita. *Batthyány utca, 80/48405. Admission: 20 Ft. adults, 10 Ft. children. Open Apr.–Aug., Tues.–Sun. 10–5.*

Just outside the Abbey complex, a pair of contemporary statues offers a startling contrast. Imre Varga's reverent 1972 statue of King Andras I is called *The Founder*; Amerigo Tot's strikingly modern 1970 abstraction is irreverently titled *His Majesty the Kilowatt.*

Time Out Next to the Abbey is the **Rege Cukrászda,** a pastry shop and café that offers not only fresh and creamy desserts but a panoramic view of Lake Balaton from its terrace.

Descend the stairs into the village, and along its main Pisky promenade you will find the **House of Folk Art,** a crafts store built in the local slope-roofed style with a charming arched porch. Next door is the **Open-air Museum of Ethnography,** an unlikely ensemble of old houses: a potter's shed with a local artist-in-residence, a winegrowing exhibition, a display of agricultural implements, a farmhouse with exquisitely carved peasant furniture, and the former house of the Fishermen's Guild with an ancient boat (used until 1934) parked inside. *Szabad tér 1. Admission: 30 Ft. adults, 15 Ft. children. Open May–Oct., Wed.–Mon. 9–6.*

Just north of the House of Folk Art is **Visszhang domb** (Echo Hill), where as many as 16 syllables used to bounce back off the Abbey wall. Nowadays, with the inroads of traffic and construction, you'll have to settle for a two-second echo, but it's still impressive.

Time Out You can practice projecting from the terraces of the **Echo Restaurant,** an inn atop Echo Hill. Whet your whistle with anything from a cup of coffee to fogas, carp, and catfish specialties.

Among the summer houses along the waterfront near Tihany's boat landing stands a neo-Baroque (1926–27) ensemble of buildings belonging to the **Biological Research Institute** of the Hungarian Academy of Sciences. The institute studies questions pertaining to the Balaton: marine biology, geology, botany, and zoology of the surrounding region. Next door, the former **Summer Home of the Habsburg Archduke Joseph,** more recently a Communist party vacation house, has a fine park with cypress trees, conifers, and gingkoes. In Kossuth Lajos utca is the **Institute of Geophysics** and above the town on Cser Hill is the institute's **Geophysical Observatory,** built without the use of any iron. No metal may be brought within 500 meters (1,640 feet) of the observatory; nor may the building be approached without special permission from the institute below. The whole peninsula is a research scientist's delight.

Footpaths connect the entire peninsula, allowing visitors to climb the small hills on its west side for splendid views of the area. If you climb its highest hill, the **Csúcshegy,** 232 meters (761 feet) high, in midsummer, you'll find the land below carpeted with purple and the air filled with the fragrance of lavender. Introduced from France into Hungary, lavender thrives on the lime-rich soil and strong sunshine of Tihany, where its essence is now stronger than in its native land. The **State Lavender and Medicinal Herb Farm** at Csúcshegy (traversed by the red walking trail from the port of Tihany) supplies the Hungarian pharmaceutical and cosmetics industries.

Highway 71, the main street of Balatonfüred, is also the shore road around the north, east, and west rims of Lake Balaton. Follow it west 7 kilometers (4.3 miles) from Balatonfüred past ➌ the turnoff for Tihany to the charming village of **Aszófő,** which dates to Roman times. Its restored ruin of a 13th-century late-**Romanesque Church,** notable for the arched gable of its facade, was itself built upon the remains of a Roman building; there is a pleasant park nearby. The neo-Classical **St. Ladislas Church** (1832–34) has a Baroque altar and an Empire-style pulpit. The town's vineyards are under landmark preservation because of the **Vörösmáli pincesor,** a row of barrel-vaulted wine cellars with Baroque decorations. Built in the 19th century, they stand behind buildings that house winepresses. Aszófő also has a fine campground (*see* Lodging, *below*) and a big wooden mill wheel that, alas, no longer turns.

Swallow your disappointment, for **Örvényes,** only 2 kilometers (1¼ miles) farther on, has the only working **Water Mill** in the Balaton region. Built in the 18th century, it still grinds grain into flour while serving as a museum as well. In the miller's room is a collection of folk art, woodcarvings, pottery, furniture, and pipes. *Admission: 20 Ft. adults, 10 Ft. children. Open June–mid-Sept., daily 10–6.*

Near the mill, a statue of St. John of Nepomuk stands on a Baroque stone bridge built in the 18th century. On a hill near the mill and road are the ruins of a Romanesque church; only its chancel has survived, and it was given a roof in 1959. On the town's only street is the Baroque Church of St. Imre, built in the late-18th century.

❹ **Balatonudvari,** 1 kilometer (½ mile) to the west, is a pleasant beach resort with a 13th-century **Catholic Church** (on a low hill near the highway) that has retained its Romanesque structure and apse, though the choir and tower were rebuilt in neo-Classical style. A **Reformed Church** (1790) has a gabled porch and late-Baroque characteristics. The **Cemetery** at the eastern end of the village has been declared a national shrine for its heart-shaped tombstones carved from white limestone at the turn of the 19th century. Balatonudvari's beach itself is at **Kiliántelep,** 2 kilometers (1¼ miles) to the west.

❺ The thriving beach resort of **Balatonakali,** 3 kilometers (1 ¾ miles) west of Kiliántelep, has ferry service and three large camping grounds. On the slopes of **Fenye-hegy** above the town are vineyards (muscatel is the local specialty) lined with thatched-roofed, whitewashed stone **Cellar Wine-Press Houses** similar to those at Örvényes, if not as ornate. A 4-kilometer (2½-mile) excursion into the volcanic hills north of Balatonakali leads to the village of **Dörgicse** with the ruins of three 12th- and 13th-century churches; a ten-minute walk takes you into the strange rock formations and caves of **Ku̇-völgy** (Stone Valley) beyond which are fine mountain views.

❻ Back on Highway 71, 5 kilometers (3 miles) west of Balatonakali is **Zánka,** a popular beach resort. Its shallow water is always wavy or rippling, for nearby is the iron-rich **Verkút** (Blood Spring), which put Zánka on the map as a spa late in the 19th century. The town's Reformed Church is of medieval origin but it was rebuilt in 1786 and again a century later with various elements preserved—leaving a pulpit supported by Roman foundations and Romanesque columns. Just west of Zánka, the landscape is disfigured by a monster-sized (formerly Communist Pioneer) children's resort capable of housing 2,500 youngsters. It has its own railway station and a **Garden of Ruins** from a destroyed medieval village, the walls of which were built by the Romans. The village was discovered during an excavation in the 1960s.

❼ The centerpiece of **Balatonszepezd,** 3 kilometers (2 miles) west of Zánka, is a **Catholic Church** that combines Romanesque and Gothic features with a minimum of mid-19th-century reconstruction. Four kilometers (2½ miles) farther west is **Révfülöp,** where eight or more ferries cross the lake every day to Balatonboglar on the southern shore. The ruins of Révfülöp's 13th-century Romanesque church stand in striking contrast to the town's new railway station. Three kilometers (2 miles) inland, to the northwest, is **Ku̇vágóörs,** one of the prettiest villages of the Balaton with a fine array of cottages in the local peasant style.

❽ Beginning 3 kilometers (2 miles) after Révfülöp are the combined communities of **Balatonrendes** and **Abrahámhegy,** which form one of Lake Balaton's quieter resorts. Abrahámhegy has the north shore's only sandy beach, as well as a nudist beach. In Balatonrendes's Fo̊ utca (Main Street) is a Baroque 18th-century **Catholic Church.** Near the beach is the summer home of Endre Bajcsy-Zsilinszky, a martyr to fascism; it is now a **Memorial Museum** that may pique your curiosity after you've crossed a Bajcsy-Zsilinszky Street in virtually every Hungarian town you visit.

❾ All this, however, is prelude to the **Badacsony,** a mysterious, coffinlike basalt peak of the Balaton Highlands along the north shore. Actually, the 438-meter- (1,437-foot-) high Mount Badacsony, its slopes rising from the lake, is an extinct volcano flanked by smaller cone-shaped hills. The masses of lava that coagulated here created bizarre and beautiful rock formations. At the upper edge, 55- to 61-meter- (180- to 200-foot-) high basalt columns tower like organ pipes in a huge semicircle. In 1965, Hungarian conservationists won a major victory that ended the quarrying of basalt from Mount Badacsony, which is now a protected nature-preservation area.

The land below has been tilled painfully and lovingly for centuries. There are vineyards everywhere and splendid wine in every inn and tavern. In descending order of dryness, the best-loved Badacsony white wines are *Rizlingszilváni, Kéknyelü,* and *Szürkebarát.* Their proud producers claim that "no vine will produce good wine unless it can see its own reflection in the Balaton." They believe that it is not enough for the sun to shine on a vine; the undersides of the leaves also need light, which is reflected from the lake's mirrorlike surface. Others claim that the wine draws its strength from the fire of old volcanoes, and its color from sunlight on the lake.

Administratively, Badacsony is a collective name that includes not just the mountain, but also five settlements at its foot. Boats and trains deliver you to **Badacsony-Üdülötelep** (Badacsony Resort), where sightseeing could start with a visit to the **József Egry Memorial Museum,** formerly the home and studio of an evocative painter of Balaton landscapes. *Egry sétány 52. Admission: 20 Ft. adults, 10 Ft. children. Open May–Oct., Tues.–Sun. 10-6.*

You can start up the mountain by car or by infrequent bus, or plod uphill on foot along **Szegedy Róza út.** This steep street is paved with basalt stones and is flanked by vineyards and villas, while water from the Kisfaludy Spring flows downhill along the side of the road. This is the place to get acquainted with the writer Sándor Kisfaludy and his beloved bride from Badacsony, Róza Szegedy, to whom he dedicated his love poems. At the summit of her street is **Róza Szegedy's Home,** a Baroque winepress house built in 1790 on such a grand scale—with thatched roof, gabled wall, six semicircular arcades, and an arched and pillared balcony running the length of the four raftered upstairs rooms—that the Szegedy family would move in for the wine harvest. It was here that the hometown girl met the visiting bard from Budapest. The house is now a memorial museum to both of them, furnished much the way it was when he was doing his best work immortalizing his two true loves, the Badacsony and his wife. *Szegedy Róza út. Admission: 20 Ft. adults, 10 Ft. children. Open Mar.–Oct., Tues.–Sun. 10-5.*

Nearby are a **Bormúzeum** (Wine Museum) built of basalt and offering wine-tastings as well as the **Museum of the Badacsony State Farm** with an exhibition of utensils, documents, photos, and charts illustrating 20 centuries of viticulture in the region. *Viktorlásház, Hegyalja út. Admission: 20 Ft. adults, 10 Ft. children. Open mid-May–mid.-Oct., Tues.–Sun. 10-4.*

Time Out A short climb up from the museums is the **Kisfaludy-ház** restaurant, once a winepress house owned by the poet's family. Its wine cellar lies directly over the Kisfaludy Spring that accompanied your upward hike, but the stellar attraction is a vast two-tiered terrace that affords a breathtaking panoramic view of virtually the entire lake. Stop for a snack or a drink on your way up and a meal on your way down; the grilled meats and *palacsinta* desserts are excellent, if expensive. Local meteorology buffs claim that if you can see across the lake from the Badacsony today, then tomorrow's weather will be bad—and, just in case, the terrace is lined with enough straw beach umbrellas to equip a Caribbean resort.

Serious summitry begins behind the Kisfaludy House at the **Rózsakő** (Rose Stone), a flat, smooth basalt slab with many carved inscriptions. Local legend has it that if a boy and a girl sit on it with their backs to Lake Balaton, they will marry within a year. But the view is very hard to turn your back on. From here, a trail marked in yellow leads up a basalt stair to the foot of the basalt columns that stretch to the top. Steep flights of stone steps take you through a narrow gap between rocks and basalt walls until you reach a tree-lined plateau. You are now at the 424-meter (1,391-foot) level. Follow the blue triangular markings along a path to the **Kisfaludy Lookout Tower.** When you have climbed its 14-meter (46-foot) height, you have scaled Mount Badacsony. Even with time out for rests and views, the ascent from the Rose Stone should take less than an hour.

If you rejoin the railroad or Highway 71 westbound after an adventure in the Badacsony, the village of **Szigliget,** formerly an island, is 11 kilometers (7 miles) away by the coast road but only 5 kilometers (3 miles) by train. Towering over the town is the ruin of the 13th-century **Óvár** (Old Castle), also known as "The Queen's Skirt" because it seems to spread out like crinoline. A fortress so well protected that it was never taken by the Turks, it was demolished in the early 18th century by Habsburgs fearful of rebellions. Down in the village, the Romanesque remains of the **Avas Church** from the Arpad dynasty still retain a 12th-century basalt tower with stone spire. The **Esterházy Summer Mansion** in the main square, Fő tér, was built in the 18th century and rebuilt in neo-Classical style in the 19th. Lately a holiday retreat for writers, it has a 10-hectare (25-acre) park with yews, willows, walnuts, pines, and more than 500 kinds of ornamental trees and shrubs; apply for permission at the front office. Szigliget also has a fine array of thatch-roof winepress houses.

From Szigliget or Badacsony, you can travel 11 kilometers (7 miles) north by bus or car to **Tapolca,** the chief city of the region. It has a fine square, **Batsányi tér,** built around an old mill pond. The mill itself is now the **Hotel Gabriella,** which retains its original architectural style. In the square, too, is a **Parish Church** of medieval origin with a 15th-century Gothic chancel, though the church was enlarged and rebuilt in Baroque style in the 18th century. A statue of the Holy Trinity stands in front of it.

If you stay on the shore, continuing west 10 kilometers (6 miles) from Szigliget, you reach **Balatongyörök,** a busy resort with three beaches; a **Roman Spring**; and a pine-covered hillside, the **Szépkilátó** (Belvedere), planted by Prince Taszilo Festetics von Tolna for his English wife, the Duchess of Hamilton. **Vonyarc-vashegy,** 4 kilometers (2½ miles) farther west, has a wine shop and restaurant, the **Helikon Tavern,** converted from one of

Prince Tassilo's wine cellars. In the village cemetery is a small neo-Classical **Szentkereszt Kápolna** (Holy Cross Chapel) with gabled facade and tower.

⑬ You are now approaching **Keszthely,** the largest town on the north shore. Keszthely offers a rare combination of historic cultural center and restful summer resort; its municipal charter dates from 1404. Its Gothic **Parish Church** (on Kossuth Lajos utca), built in 1386, was rebuilt and embellished several times (some 15th-century frescoes were recently revealed in the interior). The **Petho House** (at Kossuth Lajos utca 22), a striking town house of medieval origin, was rebuilt in Baroque style with a handsome arcaded gallery over its courtyard. In 1830, the house was the birthplace of Karl Goldmark, who composed the opera, *The Queen of Sheba.* Around the corner at Georgikon utca 20 is the building of the **Georgikon Academy of Agriculture,** founded in 1797 by Count Gyorgy Festetics. Now a university, it has become the agricultural headquarters of southwestern Hungary. Just around the corner is the **Georgikon Farm Museum,** which shows the school's history and development. *Bersényi utca 67. Admission: 20 Ft. adults, 10 Ft. children. Open Apr.–Oct., Tues.–Sat. 10–5, Sun. 10–6.*

Near the railroad station and housed in an imposing neo-Baroque building (1928), the **Balaton Museum** contains rich and varied exhibits of regional history, ethnography, folk art, and painting. *Múzeum utca 2, tel. 82/12351. Admission: 20 Ft. adults, 10 Ft. children. Open May–Oct., Tues.–Sun. 10–6; Nov.–Apr., Tues.–Sun. 10–5.*

The jewel of Keszthely is the magnificent **Festetics Palace,** one of the finest Baroque complexes in Hungary. Begun around 1745, it was the seat of the enlightened and philanthropic Festetics dynasty, which had acquired Keszthely six years earlier. The palace's distinctive churchlike tower and more than 100 rooms were added between 1883 and 1887, and the interior is exceedingly lush. The **Helikon Library** in the south wing contains some 52,000 volumes and precious codices and documents of Festetics family history, but it can also be admired for its carved-oak furniture and collection of etchings and paintings. Chamber and orchestral concerts are held in the **Mirror Gallery** ballroom or, in summer, in the courtyard. The palace opens onto a splendid park lined with rare plants and fine sculptures. *Szabadsag utca 1, tel. 82/12910. Admission: 20 Ft. adults, 10 Ft. children. Open Apr.–June and Sept., Tues.–Sun. 10–6; July–Aug., Tues.–Sun. 9–7; Oct.–Mar., Tues.–Sun. 9–5.*

⑭ Six kilometers (3½ miles) northwest of Keszthely is the spa of **Héviz** with the largest natural curative thermal lake in Europe. **Lake Héviz** covers nearly 50,000 square meters (60,000 square yards) with warm water that never grows cooler than 33–35 C (91.4–95 F) in summer and 30–32 C (86–89.6 F) in winter, thus allowing year-round bathing, particularly in the part of the lake that is covered by a roof and looks like a racetrack grandstand. The vast spa park houses hospitals, sanatoriums, hotels, and a casino. The 86-million liters (23-million gallons) of mineral-rich water gushed forth daily by the lake's 36.5-meter- (120-foot-) deep crater (the lake's water changes completely every 28 hours) are considered helpful for locomotor and certain gastric diseases.

Highway 71 turns south along the western rim of Lake Balaton at Keszthely. At **Fenékpuszta,** about 8 kilometers (5 miles) south of Keszthely, lie the ruins of the Roman settlement of **Valcum** and a three-naved early Christian **Basilica** from the fourth century.

The largest river feeding the Balaton, the Zala, enters the lake at its southwestern corner. On either side there is a vast swamp, formerly part of the lake. Known as **Kis-Balaton** (Little Balaton), some 1,400 hectares (almost 3,500 acres) of marshland were put under nature preservation in 1949. In 1953, a bird-watching station was opened nearby, and ornithologists have found some 80 breeds nesting among the reeds, many of them rare for this region. The white egret is the most treasured species. The area can be visited only by special permission of the National Office of Environmental Conservation—Ornithological Institute (Országos Környezet-és Térmészetvédelmi Hivatal—Madártani Intézet) in the capital (Költő utca 21, H-1121 Budapest) or the gateway city to the Balaton area (Tolbuhin utca 31, H-8201 Veszprém). The Kis-Balaton is entered near where Highway 71 ends its trip around the lake and yields to Highway 76 continuing south.

Tour 2: The Southern Shore

There are fewer sights along this side of the lake, just an almost unbroken chain of summer resorts. The water is shallow, and you can walk for almost a mile before it deepens. This makes it ideal for children and their parents, if not for serious swimmers. The water warms up to 25°C (77°F) in summer.

Highway (sometimes streamlined Motorway) 7 traverses this side of the water and takes over from Highway 71 (which circles the rest of the lake) near **Balatonbéreny,** a village settled during the Arpád dynasty. Bronze Age and Roman relics have been unearthed here. The Roman Catholic **Parish Church** at Kossuth Lajos utca 58 dates to the 14th and 15th centuries, and though it was rebuilt in Baroque style in 1733, it retains numerous Gothic features: pointed arches of the chancel, clergy seats, and a tabernacle. There is an excellent view of the Keszthely Hills across the lake. There is also a nudist campsite here; the identifying initials (FKK for Freie Körper-Kultur) are the same, but Hungarian nudists are much more reticent than their German and Austrian colleagues, who like to come out and wave at every passing boat.

It's worth making a 5-kilometer (3-mile) detour to the southwest to the railway junction of **Balatonszentgyoŕgy** to see **Csillagvár** (Star Castle), built in the 1820s as a hunting lodge for László, the Festetics family's eccentric. Though it is not star-shaped inside, wedge-shaped projections on the ground floor give the outside this effect. Today it is a museum of 16th- and 17th-century life in the border fortresses of the Balaton and is worth exploring for its fine cut-stone stairs and deep well, from which drinking water is still drawn. (Refreshments are available in the adjoining ex-stable.) *Irtási dűlő, tel. 84/77–193. Admission: 20 Ft. adults, 10 Ft. children. Open Mar.–Apr. and Sept.–Oct., Tues.–Sun. 9–5; May–Aug., Tues.–Sun. 9–7.*

Downtown, almost 3 kilometers (2 miles) away, is another architecturally interesting museum, the beautifully furnished **Talpasház** (House on Soles), so named because its upright beams are encased in thick foundation boards. The house is filled not only with exquisite antique peasant furniture, textiles, and pottery but also with the work of contemporary local folk artists; some of their work is for sale on the premises. *Csillagvár utca 64. Admission: 20 Ft. adults, 10 Ft. children. Open mid-Apr.–May and Sept.–mid-Oct., Tues.–Sun. 9–12:30 and 1–5; mid-May.–Aug., Tues.–Sun. 9–7.*

⑱ Back on Route 7, **Balatonmáriafürdő** is a quiet family resort established in the 1960s. Set among vineyards, it has an excellent beach stretching along 10 kilometers (6 miles) of lakeshore.

⑲ The next community, **Balatonfenyves,** stands near the **Nagyberek,** an old bay of Lake Balaton that clogged and dammed itself over the centuries into an 11,500-hectare (almost 28,500-acre) marshland. Since 1950, however, with pumping, canalization, and planting of woodland strips, some three-quarters of the Nagyberek has been reclaimed and turned into arable land. The **Nagyberek State Farm,** established on the drained marshland, specializes in livestock and game. Every year, it markets half a million pheasants and wild ducks.

⑳ With seven beaches stretching 7 kilometers (almost 4½ miles) along the shore, **Fonyód** is second only to Siófok among the most-developed resorts on the south shore of the lake. Vacationers from Pecs, 90 kilometers (56 miles) to the southeast, particularly favor Fonyód for their summer homes. An ancient settlement where late Stone Age and Bronze Age tools as well as Roman ruins have been excavated, Fonyód sits at the base of a twin-peaked hill rising directly from the shore. Atop one of the peaks, **Vár-hegy,** 233 meters (764 feet) high, stood an important fortress in Turkish times. Only its trenches and the foundation walls of a Romanesque church still stand, but this Castle Hill is worth climbing just for the view from the former courtyard of its crowning ruin. You look across the lake almost directly at Badacsony and, off in the distance to the left, Keszthely.

㉑ An interesting excursion from Fonyód can be made to **Buzsák,** 16 kilometers (10 miles) to the south. This village is famous for its colorful folk art, unique peasant needlework, and fine carving, mostly by shepherds. Today's products can be bought in local shops, but earlier masterworks are displayed in the **Regional House** museum, housed in three venerable, well-decorated rustic buildings. *Tanács tér 7. Admission: 20 Ft. adults, 10 Ft. children. Open mid-May–end of May and Sept.–mid-Oct., Tues.–Sun. 9–5; June–Aug., Tues.–Sun. 9–7. On Mondays and from mid-Oct. to mid-May, visits can be made by prior arrangement.*

㉒ Returning to Route 7, travel 10 kilometers (6 miles) east from Fonyód to the communities of Balatonboglár and Balatonlelle, which were united in 1979 into one municipality called **Boglárlelle.** (At the rate the resorts are mushrooming, they may soon merge into a minimegalopolis with Fonyód, too.)

Balatonboglár, mentioned as a community as early as 1211, is, along with Fonyód, the only other place on the south shore with hills by the lake. Eruptions of basalt tuff (stratified volcanic detritus) created these hills: At 165 meters (541 feet), Balatonboglár's highest, **Vár-hegy,** is 68 meters (223 feet) lower than Fonyód's peak of the same name. Near its summit are the double ramparts of early Iron Age defensive **Earthworks** as well as the foundation walls of a Roman watchtower. There is a good view from the spherical **Xantus Lookout Tower.** Atop the smaller **Sándor-hegy,** the crater of the tuff volcano is still visible. On **Temető-domb** (Cemetery Hill), two gaudy chapels with a sculpture garden catch the eye: The **Red Chapel** was built in 1856 and the **Blue Chapel** in 1892, both in a multitude of styles. They are the scene of an annual summer art show. *Kápolna köz. Admission: 20 Ft. adults, 10 Ft. children. Open June–mid-Sept., Tues.–Sun. 9–8.*

There are many fine houses in the village; one neo-Classical (1834) mansion is headquarters of a huge State Wine Farm and Research Station that supplies much of Hungary and Europe with Balaton wines. The village is separated from the beach resort by railroad tracks and Route 7. Frequent ferries to Révfülöp offer quick transport to the north shore.

Balatonlelle is a busy resort with some interesting modern architecture such as the **Trade Unions' Holiday Home** on Köztársaság út. It also has a few elegant homes. In the garden of a villa at Szent Istvan utca 38 is a 300-year-old **willow tree;** the oldest in Hungary, it is 7 meters (23 feet) in circumference. The annual meeting of woodcarving folk artists is held in the antebellum-looking 1838 neo-Classical **House of Culture** at Kossuth Lajos utca 2.

㉓ Balatonszemes is an older established lakeside resort with a town history dating to the 14th century. Now a school, the former **Hunyady Mansion** on Gárdonyi Géza utca was built in Baroque style in the second half of the 18th century, as was the former **Granary** opposite it. The **Parish Church** at Fő utca 23 was built in Gothic style in the 15th century, and some of its ornamented windows and the buttressed walls of the chancel still survive. Its richly decorated pastophorium is from 1517. But a unique attraction of Balatonszemes is its **Bagolyvár** (Owl Castle), an eccentric stronghold with many turrets. It was built by an Italian architect at the beginning of this century on the site of an old Turkish fort known as Fool's Castle (Bolondvár). The two southern round bastions of the old Fool's Castle are incorporated in the relatively recent Owl Castle. Balatonszemes also has a **Postal Museum** in a Baroque building where, from 1789 until early in this century, post and stagecoach horses were changed in the courtyard. Some of their old coaches are on display; the museum inside exhibits old postal equipment, uniforms, and stamps. In the summer season, there is a special post office where your mail is postmarked with an imprint representing a mail coach. *Bajcsy-Zsilinszky utca 46, tel. 84/45–160. Admission: 20 Ft. adults, 10 Ft. children. Open June–Sept., Tues.–Sun. 10–6; Oct.–Apr., Tues.–Sun. 10–2.*

㉔ Balatonszárszó, 5 kilometers (3 miles) to the east, is where the Hungarian proletarian poet Attila József—he still has as many streets named after him as Bajcsy-Zsilinszky—committed suicide in 1937 by throwing himself under a train. The boardinghouse where he spent his last weeks is now the **Attila József Memorial Museum** with extensive documentation of his life, death, and work. *József Attila utca 7. Admission: 20 Ft. adults, 10 Ft. children. Open April–Oct., Tues.–Sun. 10–6; Nov.–Mar., Tues.–Sun. 10–2.*

㉕ The second part of **Balatonföldvár's** name means "earthwork," and, indeed, this charming village was built beside an old Celtic fortification that has largely been damaged and obscured by posh villas along Petőfi Sandor utca and József Attila utca built by actors, scientists, and nobility such as the Széchenyi family. It was the Széchenyis who, in the 1890s, pioneered the development of this wilderness into a resort. The destruction of the past can perhaps be justified, if not excused, by the result: Balatonföldvár is the southern shore's most beautifully laid-out resort. Its picturebook harbor is alive with sailboats in summer; on the shore, weeping willows droop to the water as if in homage. An alley of plane trees is crowned by a superb view of the hills of Tihany across the water. Forests of flowers and spacious, symmetrical promenades all contribute to the impression that the whole town is one big park, if not the Garden of Eden. South of the railroad station, on the other side of the tracks from the water, is **Fenyves (Pinewood) Park** with an open-air theater and a brook. Campgrounds are spacious, attractive, and even luxurious; and there are excellent beaches and a wide selection of hotels, pensions, motels, and restaurants.

Four kilometers (2½ miles) south of Balatonföldvár and accessi-
㉖ ble by bus as well as auto is the village of **Köröshegy** with a single-naved 15th-century Gothic **Catholic Church**. Restored in 1969, it retains many of its original features: fortresslike Franciscan design, walls decorated with peasant carvings, a Viennese altarpiece, and a delicate rose window above a robust Gothic portal. The church has excellent acoustics and is the scene of organ, choral, and chamber concerts in summer. The **Széchenyi Mansion**, built in the French Baroque style of the late-18th century, is under landmark preservation, as is its former **Dézsma Pince** (Tithe Cellar), now operating as Borkút (Wine Well). Here the serfs had to deliver a portion of their wine harvest as payment to the landowner. There was formerly a spring inside the cellar, and it covered the walls with stalactites and stalagmites. The wines of Köröshegy (particularly the one called Italian Riesling) have been compared with those of the Moselle.

Sports and Fitness

In **Balatonfüred,** visitors can rent sailboards and sailboats on the public beach. Since motorboats are forbidden on the lake, Füred's electric water-ski towing machine, near FICC camping, is the *only* way avid skiers can get their feet wet in the entire lake. There are also several tennis courts in the Füred area, and, for those interested in less strenuous exercise, a miniature golf course (also at the FICC campgrounds). Lake Balaton is also one of the few places you can rent **bicycles** in Hungary—should you tire of swimming, sailboarding, or sunbathing. Most rental shops are near the beach or at the campgrounds. **Hiking** is particularly good near the northern resorts, around Tihany and Badascony.

Horseback riding is very popular throughout Hungary. In **Balatonfüred,** you can ride at a cost of 650 Ft. an hour at the **M & M Riding School** (Vazsónyi út 2). From the riding stables in **Felsőors,** 10 kilometers (6 miles) from Veszprem on the road to Csopak, you can hit the trail with a guide for 500 Ft. an hour;

groups of six or more can travel in more style in a horse-drawn carriage.

Dining and Lodging

Dining

Category	Cost*
Very Expensive	over 1,200 Ft.
Expensive	1,000 Ft.–1,200 Ft.
Moderate	600 Ft.–1,000 Ft.
Inexpensive	under 600 Ft.

per person, including appetizer, entrée, and dessert and excluding drinks and 10%–15% service charge

Lodging

Category	Cost*
Very Expensive	7,000 Ft.–9,000 Ft.
Expensive	6,000 Ft.–7,000 Ft.
Moderate	3,500 Ft.–6,000 Ft.
Inexpensive	1,200 Ft.–3,500 Ft.

All prices are for a standard double room, including breakfast and tax.

Aszófő
Lodging

Diana Camping. In a sylvan setting where the songs of birds are nature's best entertainment, this is the most enchanting of the Balaton's 46 campsites and, despite its capacity of 2,400 guests, one of the hardest to book because 80% of its campers (largely Austrian, German, and Dutch) come back every season. The longtime director, Aranka Minorits, is everybody's ultimate Earth Mother. Though 3 kilometers (2 miles) from the lake, this unspoiled 12-hectare (30-acre) site is nicely situated near the turnoff from Balatonfüred to Tihany. *2 km (1¼ mi) north of Hwy. 71 from village of Aszófő, H-8241, tel. 86/45013. Tent and trailer camping only; no bungalows. Facilities: shower and toilet areas, communal kitchen, grocery, restaurant, rustic wine tavern, lounge with TV, tennis courts, soccer field. No credit cards. Inexpensive.*

Badacsony
Dining

Szőlőskert. Overlooking Lake Balaton from a hillside, this venture grew like a vine into one of postcommunist Hungary's first success stories. In the late 1980s, Janos Peter leased a decaying turn-of-the-century villa from a trade union that had been abusing it and, by guaranteeing two years of hot meals free, assembled a team of workers to remodel it without pay. With private banquet rooms, the house also serves as kitchen and wine cellar for an adjoining garden restaurant. Peter the Great's empire now straddles both sides of the road above it, contining uphill through vineyards to a large modern rustic indoor-outdoor terrace restaurant with a beautiful ceramic stove and Cinemascope views of Balaton and Badacsony. Like any imperialist, Peter isn't done yet; he promises further expansion amd year-round operation. It comes almost as icing on the pancake to add that the food and drink are invariably first-rate—from the cold platters with deer salami in the villa garden to the rolled turkey breast filled with ham and mushrooms and topped with melted cheese. The *Zöldszilváni* (Green Sylvaner) wine should not be neglected. Service, mostly by Peter's family and relatives, is friendly and attentive. *Kossuth utca 16, tel. 87/31248. Reservations advised in summer. Dress: casual. No credit cards. Moderate.*

Lodging **Rozsako̎ Fogado̎.** This simple, appealing year-round pension is run by a family of young women who are eager to please and work in close cooperation with Janos Peter's neighboring Szo̎lo̎skert restaurant; either establishment will reserve the other for you. All rooms are modern with balcony. The breakfast buffet is ample and inviting. *Kossuth utca 32, H-8261, Badacsony, tel. and fax 87/31607. 17 rooms, 12 with bath. No credit cards. Inexpensive.*

Balatonakali **Mandula Csárda.** Named after its almond trees, this 19th-cen-
Dining tury vintner's house is now an elegantly rustic, totally romantic, thatch-roofed and raftered roadside inn with a shady terrace in the vineyard and Gypsy musicians serenading you as you sip delicious Balaton and Badacsony wines. It also has a playground for children. The management is fond of—and good at—organizing activities such as Gypsy, outlaw, and goulash parties as well as horseback riding and carriage outings to interesting surroundings. *On Hwy. 71, halfway between Balatonudvari and Balatonakali, H-8243, tel. 86/44511. Reservations advised. Dress: casual. No credit cards. Closed late-Sept.–early May. Moderate.*

Balatonfüred **Tölgyfa Csarda.** On a hillside away from the beach, this restau-
Dining rant takes its name from the large oak tree nearby. It's currently the most expensive restaurant in town, with a decor and menu worthy of a first-class Budapest restaurant. It's got gypsy music and a nice view, and the staff works to keep customers happy. *Meleghegy út (walk north on Jókai Mór út and turn right on Mérleg út), tel. 86/430–36. Reservations advised. Dress: casual but neat. No credit cards. Expensive.*

Baricska Csárda. Perched on a hill overlooking wine and water—its own vineyard and Lake Balaton—this rambling reed-thatched rustic inn, crawling with vines, comes alive at 6 PM and doesn't skip a beat until well past midnight. Through its many wooden-raftered rooms, vaulted cellars, and terraces (open-air and enclosed) traipse tour groups and individuals and, occasionally locals (usually on special occasions). Once they find places, they tend to stay until closing. The food is hearty yet ambitious: spicy soups in kettles, roasted trout and fogas, fish paprikash with gnocchi to soak up the rich, creamy sauce, and desserts that mix pumpkin and poppyseed with a flair known nowhere else. Try the *Baricska beles,* which lies somewhere in the realm of ecstasy between soufflé and pudding. Like the rest of the action, the Gypsy music never stops. The Riesling from the surrounding fields is dry and delicious. There is a carved wine press dating back to 1833. The inn has achieved European recognition by winning a gold medal from the International Organization of Press for Tourism and Gastronomy (FIPREGA) and a certificate pronouncing it a "Maison de Qualité." *Baricska du̎lo̎, off Hwy. 71 (Széchenyi út) behind Shell station, tel. and fax 86/43105. Reservations advised. Dress: casual. No credit cards. Closed Nov. 11–Mar. 14. Moderate.*

Hordo Csárda. Next door to Baricska, this venerable inn whose cellars once served for barbecuing sausages as well as for aging wine has an uphill fight to compete with its noted neighbor. But it has its advantages: Gypsy music, Transylvanian meat specialties, fish soup and goulashes prepared in outdoor cauldrons, and wine-tastings in September accompanied by a folklore show. The Jókai bean soup with pork and cabbage can be a meal in itself. If you have room, try the pumpkin and poppyseed strudels. *Baricska dülő, off Hwy. 71 (Széchenyi út) behind Shell station, tel. 86/43417. Reservations not necessary. Dress: casual. No credit cards. Closed Nov.–Mar. Moderate.*

Halászkert Etterem. Known as the Fisherman's Garden, this beachfront restaurant is famous for its Balaton pike perch, which tastes best when grilled over an open flame. Although food is supposed to be served only until 11 PM, with a little persuasion you can keep on ordering until after midnight. In between courses you can dance on the restaurant's outdoor dance floor. *Széchenyi 2, off Jókai Mór út, near dock, tel. 86/430–39. Reservations advised for dinner. Dress: casual but neat. No credit cards. Inexpensive.*

Lodging **Marina.** This is really two hotels and the one you prefer will be a matter of taste and price. The spiffy 12-story beachfront skyscraper from the mid-1980s costs 25% more and has much less character than the slightly run-down, low-slung, three-story Lido wing, which dates to 1970 and opens right onto the water. Lido guests can, of course, use the high-rise facilities, too, which include a large indoor swimming pool and a rooftop restaurant. Thanks to a youthful staff that is friendly, helpful, and never impersonal or condescending, even the glitzy main lobby radiates warmth and personality, and the whole Marina experience becomes virtually villagelike. *Széchenyi út 26, H-8239 Balatonfüred, tel. 86/43644, fax 86/43052. 375 rooms, 24 apartments, all with bath. Restaurant, beer tavern, bar, nightclub, boating, beach, indoor swimming pool, sauna, solarium, bowling alley. AE, DC, MC, V. Closed Oct.–Mar. (indoor pool stays open year-round). Moderate–Expensive.*

Annabella. Situated in the spa park overlooking the Tagore Promenade and Lake Balaton, this large, modern hotel offers excellent swimming and water-sports facilities. It is just around the corner from the main square in town. *Beloiannisz utca 25, H-8230 Balatonfüred, tel. 86/42222. 390 rooms; all double rooms have bath. ££. Facilities: restaurant, bar, pool. AE, DC, MC, V. Closed Oct.–Mar. Moderate.*

Füred. This 12-story lakefront hotel caters to small congresses and groups but is a pleasant place for individual guests, too. *Széchenyi út 20, H-8230 Balatonfüred, tel. 86/43033, fax 86/32622. 152 rooms with bath. Facilities: 2 restaurants, bar, coffee shop, wine cellar, tennis court, bowling alley, sailing, parking. AE, DC, MC, V. Moderate.*

Margaréta. This attractive apartment hotel stands across the street from the lakefront Hotel Marina, and its guests are expected to use the Marina's facilities. It is smaller and more intimate than some of its neighbors, and its restaurant is popular locally. All apartments have kitchen, balcony, phone, TV, and radio. *Széchenyi út 29, H-8230 Balatonfüred, tel. 86/43824, fax 86/43052. 52 apartments, all with bath. Facilities: restaurant, bar, snack bar, parking, beach, fishing. AE, DC, MC, V. Moderate.*

Arany Csillag. This is the choice if you've had enough of Hungary's more modern accommodations. The Golden Star is a simple and pleasantly old-fashioned hotel in the center of town, across

from the park. *Zsigmond utca 1, tel. 86/43466. 79 rooms, none with bath. Facilities: restaurant. No credit cards. Inexpensive.*
27th FICC Rally Camping Site. At water's edge next door to the Hotel Marina, there is nothing primitive about Hungary's biggest and best campsite, open year-round with bungalows that can be heated in winter. On 27 hectares (67 acres) with facilities to accommodate 3,500 people (including tourists without tents or vehicles), it is a self-contained village with its own post office, beauty parlor, self-service laundry, and supermarket. *Széchenyi út 24, H-8230 Balatonfüred, tel. 86/43823. Facilities: restaurant, cafés, snack bars, bathing, boating, waterskiing, water chute, tennis courts, bowling alley, minigolf, sauna, solarium, fishing. No credit cards. Inexpensive.*

Balatonmáriafürdő
Lodging

Hotel Maria. This lakeshore hotel, in a three-story modern building reconstructed in 1986, has its own private beach and easy access to nearby tennis courts and other sports activities. *Rakoczi út 1, Box 37, H-8847, tel. 84/76038 and 76039. 94 rooms with bath. Facilities: bar, breakfast lounge, parking, hotel taxi. AE, DC, MC, V. Closed Oct.–Apr. Moderate.*

Fonyód
Dining

Presház Csárda. Above the remains of Fonyód Castle, the driveway leading to a four-pillared veranda is so imposing that you may expect to be greeted by Scarlett O'Hara, but behind the noble facade of this "winepress-house inn" is a thatch-roofed structure typical of the region and a wine cellar 22 meters (24 yards) long, all with cozy rustic furnishings. Hungarian food and local wines are excellent. *Lenke utca 22. No credit cards. Moderate.*

Héviz
Lodging

Aqua Thermal Hotel. This large, luxurious spa-hotel has its own thermal baths and physiotherapy unit, plus a full dental service. It is open year-round. *Kossuth Lajos utca 13–15, H-8380, tel. 82/18947, fax 82/18970, telex 35-247. 230 rooms with bath. Facilities: restaurant, bar, pool, sauna, solarium, hairdresser, medical services. AE, DC, MC, V. Expensive.*
Thermal Hotel Héviz. Very similar in its offerings to its neighbor the Aqua Thermal (*see above*), this large spa-hotel has the additional attraction of a casino. *Kossuth Lajos utca 9-11, H-8380, tel. 82/18130, fax 82/18442, telex 35-286. 203 rooms with bath. Facilities: restaurant, bar, pool, sauna, thermal baths, solarium, medical services. AE, DC, MC, V. Expensive.*

Keszthely
Dining

Gösser Söröző. This centrally located beer garden keeps long hours and plenty of beer on tap for its mostly Austrian clientele. The food is better than you might guess judging just from the touristy atmosphere. Aside from barroom snacks, the menu features Hungarian specialties, such as *gulyasleves* (goulash), *gombás rostélyos* (a mushroom dish), and *töltöttpaprika* (stuffed paprika). The only vegetarian option is salad. In summer, German beer-hall music starts live at 6. *Kossuth Lajos út 35, just north of Fő tér, tel. 82/22–65. Wheelchair access. Open daily 9 AM–midnight, later hours weekends and summer. No reservations. Dress: casual. Inexpensive.*
Panoráma Csárda. On the main highway in the small village of Balatongyörök, this restaurant lives up to its name, providing a stunning panorama of the lake from its hillside location. Even the hill it's built on is called Szépkilátó (beautiful view). Once you've chosen dishes such as Wiener schnitzel or pork with dumplings, you can hang out here for quite a while, enjoying the view and writing postcards. Most of the customers are tourists. The view makes it worth the taxi or bus ride out here.

Balatongyörök, Hwy. 71. Bus from Keszthely to Tapolca stops in front of restaurant. Wheelchair access. No reservations. Dress: casual. Closed Nov.–Feb. Inexpensive.

Lodging **Helikon Castle.** Usually reserved for small, secluded conferences, 19 guest rooms within Keszthely's grandest sight are occasionally available to individuals. *Szabadsag utca 1, H-8360, tel. 82/15039. 19 rooms with bath. Facilities: restaurant, bar, conference room. No credit cards. Expensive.*

Helikon Hotel. This large and comfortable lakeside hotel is convenient and popular with groups. *Balaton-part 5, H-8360, tel. 82/18944, fax 82/18403. 240 rooms with bath. Facilities: restaurant, bar, pool, fitness center. AE, DC, MC, V. Expensive.*

Amazon. Behind a beautiful facade in the style of late-18th-century French architecture is this simple tourist hostel in the center of town. *Szabadsag utca, H-8360, tel. 82/122–48. 16 rooms, half with bath. Facilities: restaurant, bar, nightclub. No credit cards. Inexpensive.*

Tapolca **Aspa Panzio.** This is a comfortable pension in the center of
Lodging town. *Kossuth Lajos utca 19, H-8300, tel. 871/1695. 9 rooms with bath. Facilities: restaurant, bar, tennis, sailing, horseback riding, bowling, medical services. No credit cards. Inexpensive.*

Gabriella Hotel. This is a small, charming hotel in a converted mill on the main square, which is also the main attraction of this road and rail junction. *Batsanyi tér 7, H-8300, tel. 871/2642. 14 rooms. Facilities: restaurant. No credit cards. Inexpensive.*

Tihany **Sport.** Beautifully situated near the Tihany boat landing, this
Dining first-class garden restaurant faces south to afford a panoramic view of Lake Balaton. Large bay windows allow similar views from inside the 1920s main house, where the back wall is richly painted by women folk artists from Kalocsa. Fish soup is a main-course specialty. There is disco dancing at night. *Fürdőtelep 34, tel. 86/48251. Reservations recommended. Dress: informal. AE, DC, MC, V. Open Easter–Sept. Expensive.*

Fogas. Named after a type of perch native to Lake Balaton, the restaurant specializes in this and other fish dishes. It is right at the northern end of Tihany village. *Kossuth utca 1, tel. 86/48658. No reservations. No credit cards. Moderate.*

Halásztánya. The relaxed atmosphere and Gypsy music in the evening help contribute to the popularity of the Halásztánya, which specializes in fish. *Visszhang utca 11. No telephone. No reservations. Closed Nov.–Mar. Moderate.*

HBH Kolostor sörözö. At the foot of the abbey steps, this new beer restaurant offers striking views of the church complex above, shimmeringly illuminated through the trees at night. There is an outdoor grill in the garden. Inside this spacious chalet, which seats 400, is a glass-enclosed, working brewery, and during the day you can watch men in blue smocks sipping seriously and puckering for quality control. It is all very thirst-provoking, as are the fish specialties that include eel paprikash; trout with almonds; the Balaton's ubiquitous pike-perch, *fogas;* and its young, *süllő,* served in filets with tiny crayfish and dill sauce. *Kossuth utca 14, tel. 86/48408. Reservations advised in summer. Dress: casual. AE, MC, V. Open Easter through New Year's Eve. Moderate.*

Lodging **Club Tihany.** A year-round resort complex of Club Med proportions at the tip of the peninsula, this 13-hectare (32-acre) holiday village calls itself an "island of opportunities" for sports and recreation. It boasts facilities for bathing, boating, surfing, tennis, squash, badminton, Ping-Pong, bowling, biking, hiking, horseback riding, fishing, sauna, fitness, and gymnastics. Housing is in 161 luxury bungalows that offer a choice of architecture—suburban A-frame, modern atrium, or slope-roofed minifarmhouse (all with kitchen facilities)—as well as in the inappropriately Miami Beachlike white-Lego main building, the Hotel Tihany, which has 330 rooms and a swimming pool in the lobby. Scattered around the premises are two restaurants, two beer halls, three bars, a wine restaurant festooned with antlers and other hunt trophies, and, in the center of the complex, the lovely Lavender Restaurant, with muted flower decor and beef specialties. *Rév utca 3, H-8237 Tihany, tel. 86/48088, fax 86/48110. 300 rooms with bath. Facilities: restaurants, pools, squash, tennis, miniature golf. AE, DC, MC, V. Expensive.*

Veszprém **Bakony.** An elegant restaurant in the center of town, Bakony
Dining specializes in fish dishes and has a wide-ranging menu. *Lenin tér 2, tel. 80/12–215. No reservations. No credit cards. Moderate.*

★ **Vadásztanya.** The Hunter's Den is just a little southwest of the town center but worth the trip if you want to experience the old-fashioned charm of a small provincial Hungarian restaurant. The decor could be called Cozy Traditional and the fish and game specialties are perennial favorites. *József Attila utca 22, tel. 80/12–495. No reservations. No credit cards. Moderate.*

Lodging **Veszprém.** This modern and comfortable hotel in the center of town is convenient to most of the major sights. *Budapesti utca 6, tel. 80/12345. Facilities: restaurant. No credit cards. Moderate.*

Hungarian Vocabulary

	English	Hungarian	Pronunciation
Common Greetings	Hello (good day).	Jó napot./Jó napot kivánok.	**yoh** nuh-poht/**yoh** nuh-poht **kee**-vah-nohk
	Good-bye.	Viszontlátásra.	**vee**-sohnt-lah-tahsh-ruh
	Hello/Good-bye (informal).	Szervusz.	**ser**-voos
	Good morning.	Jó reggelt kivánok.	**yoh** reg-gelt **kee**-vah-nohk
	Good evening.	Jó estét kivánok.	**yoh** esh-tayt **kee**-vah-nohk
	Ma'am	Asszonyom	**uhs**-sohn-yohm
	Miss	Kisasszony	**keesh**-uhs-sohny
	Mr./Sir	Uram	**oor**-uhm

To address someone as Mrs., add the suffix "né" to the last name. Mrs. Kovács is then "Kovácsné." To address someone as Mr., use the word "úr" after the last name. Mr. Kovács is then "Kovács úr."

	English	Hungarian	Pronunciation
	Good morning, Mrs. Kovács/ Mr. Kovács	Jó reggelt, Kovácsné/ Kovács úr.	**yoh** reg-gelt **koh**-vahch-nay/ **koh**-vahch oor
	How are you?	Hogy van?	**hohdge** vuhn
	Fine, thanks. And you?	Jól vagyok, köszönöm. És maga?	**yohl** vuhdge-ohk **ku(r)**-su(r)-nu(r)m aysh **muh**-guh
	What is your name?	Hogy hívják?	**hohdge heev**-yahk
	What is your name (informal)?	Hogy hívnak?	**hohdge** heev-nuhk
	My name is . . .	(Name) vagyok.	**vuhdge**-ohk
	Good luck!	Jó szerencsét!	**yoh** se-ren-chayt
Polite Expressions	Please	Kérem szépen	**kay**-rem **say**-pen
	Thank you.	Köszönöm.	**ku(r)**-su(r)-nu(r)m
	Thank you very much.	Nagyon szépen köszönöm.	**nuhdge**-ohn **say**-pen **ku(r)**-su(r)-nu(r)m

This material is adapted from Living Language™ *Fast & Easy* Hungarian *(Crown Publishers, Inc.). Fast & Easy "survival" courses are available in 15 different languages, including Czech, Hungarian, Polish, and Russian. Each interactive 60-minute cassette teaches more than 300 essential phrases for travelers. Available in bookstores or call 800/733–3000 to order.*

You're welcome.	Kérem szépen.	**kay**-rem **say**-pen
You're welcome (informal).	Szivesen.	**see**-vesh-en
Yes, thank you.	Igen, köszönöm.	**ee**-gen **ku(r)**-su(r)-nu(r)m
No, thank you.	Nem, köszönöm.	**nem ku(r)**-su(r)-nu(r)m
Pardon me.	Bocsánat.	**boh**-chah-nuht
I'm sorry (sympathy, regret).	Sajnálom.	**shuhy**-nahl-ohm
I don't understand.	Nem értem.	nem **ayr**-tem
I don't speak Hungarian very well.	Nem beszélek jól magyarul.	nem **bess**-ayl-ek yohl **muh**-dgeuhr-ool
Do you speak English?	Beszél angolul?	**be**-sayl **uhn**-gohl-ool
Yes/No	Igen/Nem	**ee**-gen/nem
Speak slowly, please.	Kérem, beszéljen lassan.	**kay**-rem **bess**-ay-yen **luhsh**-shuhn
Repeat, please.	Ismételje meg, kérem.	**eesh**-may-tel-ye meg **kay**-rem
I don't know.	Nem tudom.	**nem** too-dohm
Here you are (when giving something).	Tessék.	**tesh**-shayk
Excuse me (what did you say)?	Tessék?	**tesh**-shayk
Questions What is . . . What is this?	Mi . . . Mi ez?	**mee** ez
When . . . When will they be ready?	Mikor . . . Mikor lesznek készen?	**mee**-kor **less**-nek **kayss**-en
Why . . . Why is the pastry shop closed?	Miért . . . Miért van zárva a cukrászda?	**mee**-aryt vuhn **zahr**-vuh uh **tsook**-rahss-duh
Who . . . Who is your friend?	Ki . . . Ki a barátod?	**kee** uh **buh**-raht-ohd
How . . . How do you say this in Hungarian?	Hogy . . . Hogy mondják ezt magyarul?	**hohdge mohnd**-yahk ezt **muh**-dgeuhr-ool
Which . . . Which train goes to Esztergom?	Melyik . . . Melyik vonat megy Esztergomba?	**mey**-eek **voh**-nuht **medge ess**-ter-gohm-buh
What do you want to do?	Mit akar csinálni?	**meet** uh-kuhr **chee**-nahl-nee

What do you want to do (informal)?	Mit akarsz csinálni?	**meet** uh-kuhrss **chee**-nahl-nee
Where are you going?	Hova megy?	**hoh**-vuh medge
Where are you going (informal)?	Hova mész?	**hoh**-vuh mayss
What is the date today?	Hanyadika van ma?	**huh**-nyuh-deek-uh vuhn muh
May I?	Szabad?	**suh**-buhd
May I take this?	Szabad ezt elvenni?	**suh**-buhd ezt **el**-ven-nee
May I come in?	Szabad bejönni?	**suh**-buhd **be**-yu(r)n-nee
May I take a photo?	Szabad fényképezni?	**suh**-buhd **fayn**-kayp-ez-nee
May I smoke?	Szabad dohányozni?	**suh**-buhd **doh**-hahn-yohz-nee

Directions	Where	Hol	hohl
	Excuse me, where is the . . . ?	Bocsánat, hol van a . . . ?	**boh**-chah-nuht **hohl** vuhn uh
	Excuse me, where is Castle Hill?	Bocsánat, hol van a vár?	**boh**-chah-nuht **hohl** vuhn uh **vahr**
	Where is the toilet?	Hol van a toálet (WC)?	**hohl** vuhn uh **toh**-ah-let (**vay**-tsay)
	Where is the bus stop?	Hol van a buszmegallo?	**hohl** vuhn uh **booss**-meg-ahl-loh
	Where is the subway station?	Hol van a metro?	**hohl** vuhn uh **met**-roh
	Go	Menjen	**men**-yen
	To the right	Jobbra	**yohb**-bruh
	To the left	Balra	**buhl**-ruh
	Straight ahead	Egyenessen előre	**edge**-en-esh-shen **e**-lu(r)-re
	At the end of the street	Az utca végén	uhz **oot**-suh **vay**-gayn
	The first left	Az első balra	uhz **el**-shu(r) **buhl**-ruh
	Near	Közel	**ku(r)z**-el
	It's near here.	Közel van ide.	**ku(r)z**-el vuhn **ee**-de
	Turn	Forduljon	**fohr**-dool-yohn
	Go back.	Menjen vissza.	**men**-yen **vees**-suh
	Next to . . .	. . . mellett	. . . **mel**-lett

	Next to the post office	A pósta mellett	uh **pohsh**-tuh **mel**-lett
	It's very simple.	Nagyon egyszerű.	**nuhdge**-ohn **edge**-ser-ew
At the Hotel	Room	Szoba	**soh**-buh
	I would like . . .	Kérek . . .	**kay**-rek
	I would like a room.	Kérek egy szobát.	**kay**-rek edge **soh**-baht
	For one person	Egy személyre	edge **sem**-ay-re
	For two people	Két személyre	kayt **sem**-ay-re
	For how many nights?	Hány éjszakára?	**hahny**-suhk-ah-ruh
	For tonight	Ma éjszakára	**muh** ay-suhk-ah-ruh
	For two nights	Két éjszakára	kayt **ay**-suhk-ah-ruh
	For a week	Egy hétre	edge **hayt**-re
	Do you have a different room?	Van egy másik szoba?	vuhn edge **mahsh**-eek **soh**-buh
	With a bath	Fürdőszobával	**fewr**-du(r)-soh-bah-vuhl
	With a shower	Zuhanyal	**zoo**-huhn-yuhl
	With a toilet	WC-vel	**vay**-tsay vel
	The key, please.	Kérem a kulcsot.	**kay**-rem uh **koolch**-oht
	How much is it?	Mennyibe kerül?	**men**-yee-be **ker**-ewl
	My bill, please.	Kérem a számlát.	**kay**-rem uh **sahm**-laht
At the Restaurant	Café	Kávéház	**kah**-vay-hahz
	Restaurant	Étterem	**ayt**-ter-rem
	Where is a good restaurant?	Hol van egy jó étterem?	hohl vuhn edge **yoh** ayt-ter-rem
	Reservation	Rezerváció	**re**-zer-vah-tsee-oh
	Table for two	Asztal két személyre	**uhss**-tuhl kayt **sem**-ay-re
	Waiter	Pincér	**peen**-sayr
	Waitress	Pincérnő	**peen**-sayr-nu(r)

(Waiters and waitresses are more likely to respond to the request "Kérem" (**kay**-rem), which means "please.")

	I would like the menu, please.	Kérem az étlapot.	**kay**-rem uhz **ayt**-luhp-oht
	The wine list, please.	Kérem a borlapot.	**kay**-rem uh **bohr**-luhp oht

The beverage list, please.	Kérem az itallapot.	**kay**-rem uhz **ee**-tuhl-luhp-oht
Appetizers	Előételek	**el**-u(r)-ay-tel-ek
Main course	Főétel	**fu(r)**-ay-tel
Dessert	Deszert	**dess**-ert
What would you like to drink?	Mit tetszik inni?	meet **tet**-seek **een**-nee
A beer, please.	Egy sört kérek.	edge shurt **kay**-rek
Wine, please.	Bort kérek.	**bohrt kay**-rek
The specialty of the day	A mai ajánlat	uh **muh**-ee **uhy**-ahn-luht
What would you like?	Mit tetszik parancsolni?	meet **tet**-seek **puh**-ruhn-chohl-nee
Can you recommend a good wine?	Tudna ajánlani egy finom bort?	**tood**-nuh **uhy**-ahn-luhn-ee edge **fee**-nohm bohrt
I didn't order this.	Ezt nem rendeltem.	ezt **nem ren**-del-tem
That's all, thanks.	Ez minden, köszönöm.	Ez **meen**-den **ku(r)**-su(r)-nu(r)m
The check, please.	Kérem szépen a számlát.	**kay**-rem **say**-pen uh **sahm**-laht
Is the tip included?	Benne van a borravallo?	**ben**-ne vuhn uh **bohr**-ruh-vuhl-loh
Breakfast	Reggeli	**reg**-gel-ee
Lunch	Ebéd	e-bayd
Supper	Vacsora	**vuh**-chohr-uh
Bon appetit.	Jó étvágyat.	**yoh** ayt-vahdge-uht
To your health!	Egészségére!	e-gayss-shayg-ay-re
Fork	Villa	**veel**-luh
Knife	Kés	kaysh
Spoon	Kanál	**kuh**-nahl
Napkin	Szalvéta	**suhl**-vay-tuh
Cup of tea	Téa	**tay**-uh
Bottle of wine	Üveg bor	**ew**-veg **bohr**
Ice	Kis jég	keesh yayg
Salt and pepper	Só és bors	shoh aysh bohrsh
Sugar	Cukor	**tsoo**-kohr
Soup	Leves	**le**-vesh
Salad	Saláta	**shuhl**-ah-tuh
Vegetables	Zöldség	**zu(r)ld**-shayg
Beef	Marhahús	**muhr**-huh-hoosh
Chicken	Csirke	**cheer**-ke

Bread	Kenyér	**ken**-yayr
Black coffee	Fekete kávé	**fe**-ke-te **kah**-vay
Coffee with milk	Tejeskávé	tey-esh-**kah**-vay
Tea with lemon	Téa citrommal	**tey**-uh **tseet**-rohm-muhl
Orange juice	Narancslé	**nuh**-ruhnch-lay
Mineral water	Ásványvíz	**ahsh**-vahn'y-veez
Another	Még egy	**mayg** ed'y
I'd like some more mineral water.	Kérek még egy ásványvízet.	**kay**-rek **meyg** ed'y **ahsh**-vahny-veez-et
I'd like some more bread and butter.	Kérek még kenyeret és vajat.	**kay**-rek mayg **ken**-yer-et aysh **vuhy**-uht
Is it very spicy?	Nagyon erős ez?	**nuhdge**-ohn e-ru(r)sh ez
May I exchange this?	Ezt kicserélhetem?	ezt **kee**-che-rayl-het-em

Numbers	0	Nulla	**nool**-luh
	1	Egy	edge
	2	Kettő	**ket**-tu(r)
	3	Három	**hah**-rohm
	4	Négy	naydge
	5	Öt	u(r)t
	6	Hat	huht
	7	Hét	hayt
	8	Nyolc	nyohlts
	9	Kilenc	**kee**-lents
	10	Tíz	teez
	11	Tizenegy	**teez**-en-edge
	12	Tizenkettő	**teez**en-ket-tu(r)
	13	Tizenhárom	**teez**-en-hah-rohm
	14	Tizennégy	**teez**-en-naydge
	15	Tizenöt	**teez**-en-u(r)t
	16	Tizenhat	**teez**-en-huht
	17	Tizenhét	**teez**-en-hayt
	18	Tizennyolc	**teez**-en-nyohlts
	19	Tizenkilenc	**teez**-en-kee-lents
	20	Húsz	hooss
	21	Huszonegy	**hooss**-ohn-edge
	22	Huszonkettő	**hooss**-ohn-ket-tu(r)
	30	Harminc	**huhr**-meents
	40	Negyven	**nedge**-ven
	50	Ötven	**u(r)t**-ven
	60	Hatvan	**huht**-vuhn
	70	Hetven	**het**-ven
	80	Nyolcvan	**nyohlts**-vuhn
	90	Kilencven	**kee**-lents-ven
	100	Száz	sahz
	1,000	Ezer	e-zer

Telling Time	What time is it?	Hány óra van?	**hahny** oh-ruh vuhn
	Midnight	Éjfél	**ay**-fayl

It is 1:00 AM.	Hajnali egy óra van.	**huhy**-nuhl-ee **edge** oh-ruh vuhn
It is 2:00 AM.	Hajnali két óra van.	**huhy**-nuhl-ee **kayt oh**-ruh vuhn
It is 9:00 AM.	Reggel kilenc óra van.	reg-gel **kee**-lents **oh**-ruh vuhn
10:00 AM	Reggel tíz óra	reg-gel **teez oh**-ruh
It is noon.	Dél van.	**dayl** vuhn
It is 1:00 PM.	Délután egy óra van.	**dayl**-oo-tahn **edge oh**-ruh vuhn
It is 6:00 PM.	Délután hat óra van.	**dayl**-oo-tahn **huht oh**-ruh vuhn
7:00 PM	Este hét óra	**esh**-te **hayt oh**-ruh
8:00 PM	Este nyolc óra	**esh**-te **nyolts oh**-ruh
Minute	Perc	perts
3:20 PM	Délután három óra húsz perc	**dayl**-oo-tahn **hah**-rohm **oh**-ruh **hooss** perts
8:30 AM	Reggel nyolc óra harminc perc	reg-gel **nyohlts oh**-ruh **huhr**-meents perts
Early morning	Hajnal	**huhy**-nuhl
Morning	Reggel	**reg**-gel
Before noon	Délelőtt	**dayl**-el-u(r)t
Afternoon	Délután	**dayl**-oo-tahn
Evening	Este	**esh**-te
Night	Éjszaka	**ay**-suhk-uh
Now	Most	mohsht
Later	Később	**kay**-shu(r)b
Immediately	Mindjárt	**meen**-dyahrt
Soon	Majd	muhyd

Days of the Week	Monday	Hétfő	**hayt**-fu(r)
	Tuesday	Kedd	ked
	Wednesday	Szerda	**ser**-duh
	Thursday	Csütörtök	**chew**-tur-tu(r)k
	Friday	Péntek	**payn**-tek
	Saturday	Szombat	**sohm**-buht
	Sunday	Vasárnap	**vuh**-shahr-nuhp
Months	January	Január	**yuh**-noo-ahr
	February	Február	**feb**-roo-ahr
	March	Március	**mahr**-tsee-oosh
	April	Április	**ah**-pree-leesh
	May	Május	**mah**-yoosh
	June	Június	**yoo**-nee-oosh

July	Július	**yoo**-lee-oosh
August	Augusztus	**ow**-goost-oosh
September	Szeptember	**sep**-tem-ber
October	Október	**ohk**-toh-ber
November	November	**noh**-vem-ber
December	December	**de**-tsem-ber

Shopping

Money	Pénz	paynz
Where is the bank?	Hol van a bank?	hohl vohn uh **buhnk**
I would like to change some money.	Szeretnék pénzt beváltani.	**Se**-ret-nayk paynzt **be**-vahl-tuh-nee
140 forints	Száznegyven forint	**Sahz**-nedge-ven **foh**-reent
1,100 forints	Ezeregyszáz forint	**e**-zer-edge-sahz **foh**-reent
Please write it down.	Kérem írja fel.	**kay**-rem **eer**-yuh fel
How can I help you?	Tessék parancsolni?	**tesh**-shayk **puh**-ruhn-chohl-nee
I would like this.	Ezt kérem.	ezt **kay**-rem
Here it is.	Tessék itt van.	**tesh**-shayk eet vuhn
Would you care for anything else?	Más valamit?	**mahsh** **vuh**-luh-meet
That's all, thanks.	Mást nem kérek, köszönöm.	mahsht nem **kay**-rek **ku(r)**-su(r)-nu(r)m
Would you accept a traveler's check?	Elfogadják az utazási csekket?	**el**-foh-guhd-yahk uhz **oot**-uhz-ahsh-ee **chek**-ket
Credit cards?	Hitelkártya?	**hee**-tel-kahr-tyuh
How much?	Mennyi?	**men**-nyee
Department store	Áruház	**ah**-roo-hahz
Bakery	Pékség	**payk**-shayg
Pastry shop	Cukrászda	**tsook**-rahz-duh
Grocery store	Élelmiszerbolt	**ayl**-el-mees-er-bohlt
Butcher's shop	Hentes	**hen**-tesh
I would like a loaf of bread.	Kérek egy kenyeret.	**kay**-rek edge **ke**-nyer-et
Bottle of white wine	Üveg fehérbor	**ew**-veg **fe**-hayr-bohr
I would like 30 dekagrams of cheese.	Kérek harminc deka sajtot.	**kay**-rek **huhr**-meents **de**-kuh **shuhy**-toht
Give me six apples.	Tessék adni hat almát.	**tesh**-shayk **uhd**-nee huht **uhl**-maht

. . . and a kilo of grapes	. . . és egy kiló szőlőt	aysh edge **kee**-loh **su(r)**-lu(r)t
Clothing	Ruha	**roo**-huh
Woman's clothing	Nőiruha	**nu(r)**-ee-roo-huh
Toys and gifts	Játék és ajándék	**yah**-tayk aysh **uh**-yahn-dayk
Folk art and embroideries	Népművészet és kézimunka	**nayp**-mew-vays-et aysh **kay**-zee-moon-kuh

The Post Office	Post office	Pósta	**pohsh**-tuh
	Where is the post office?	Hol van a pósta?	**hohl** vuhn uh **pohsh**-tuh
	Some stamps, please.	Bélyegeket kérek.	**bay**-yeg-ek-et **kay**-rek
	For letters or postcards?	Levélre vagy képeslapra?	le-**vayl**-re vuhdge **kay**-pesh-luhp-ruh
	Where are you sending them?	Hova küldi?	**hoh**-vuh **kewl**-dee
	To the United States	Az Egyesült Államokba	uhz **edge**-esh-ewlt **ahl**-luhm-ohk-buh
	Airmail	Légipósta	**lay**-gee-pohsh-tuh
	Telephone directory	Telefonkönyv	**te**-le-fohn-ku(r)nyv
	Where can I telephone?	Hol lehet telefonálni?	hohl **le**-het **te**-le-fohn-ahl-nee
	Telephone call	Telefonhívás	**te**-le-fohn-heev-ahsh
	What number, please?	Melyik telefonszámat kéri?	**me**-yeek **te**-le-fohn-sahm-uht **kay**-ree
	The line is busy.	A vonal foglalt.	uh **voh**-nuhl **fohg**-luhlt
	There's no answer, try again later.	Nincs válasz, tessék később próbálni.	neench **vah**-luhs **tesh**-shayk **kay**-shu(r)b **proh**-bahl-nee
	May I speak to . . . ?	Beszélhetek . . . ?	**be**-sayl-he-tek
	May I leave a message?	Hagyhatok üzenetet?	**huhdge**-huh-tohk ew-ze-net-et

The Airport	Where is customs?	Hol van a vám?	hohl vuhn uh **vahm**
	Where is the passport control?	Hol van az útlevélellenőrzes?	hohl vuhn uhz **oot**-le-vayl-**el**-len-ur-zesh
	Where does the baggage arrive?	Hol érkeznek a csomagok?	hohl **ayr**-kez-nek uh **choh**-muhg-ohk

Where is the departures wing?	Hol van az indulási oldal?	hohl vuhn uhz **een**-dool-ahsh-ee **ohl**-duhl
Where is the arrivals wing?	Hol van az érkezési oldal?	hohl vuhn uhz **ayr**-kez-ay-shee **ohl**-duhl
Where is a taxi?	Hol van a taxi?	hohl vuhn uh **tuhx**-ee
Where is the exit?	Hol van a kijárat?	hohl vuhn uh **kee**-yahr-uht
Is there a subway or a bus here?	Van itt metro vagy autobusz?	vuhn eet **met**-roh vuhdy **ow**-toh-boos
Stop here, please.	Kérem szépen, álljon meg itt.	**kay**-rem **say**-pen **ahl**-yohn meg eet
What is the fare to the Parliament?	Mennyi az ár a Parlementig?	**men**-yee uhz ahr uh **puhr**-le-men-teeg
What is the fare?	Mennyi a viteldíj?	**men**-yee uh **vee**-tel-dee

The Train Station

I would like a ticket, please.	Egy jegyet kérek.	edge **yedge**-et **kay**-rek
A return ticket First class	Egy retur jegy Elsö osztályú	edge **re**-toor yedge **el**-shu(r) **ohs**-tahy-oo
Do you have a timetable?	Van itt menetrend?	vuhn eet **me**-net-rend
Is there a dining car?	Van étkezőkocsi?	vuhn **ayt**-kez-u(r)-koh-chee
Sleeping car	Hálókocsi	**hah**-loh-koh-chee
Where is this train going?	Hova megy ez a vonat?	**hoh**-vuh medge ez uh **voh**-nuht
When does the train leave for Pécs?	Mikor indul a vonat Pécsre?	**mee**-kohr **een**-dool uh **voh**-nuht **paych**-re
When does the train arrive from Pecs?	Mikor érkezik a vonat Pécsröl?	**mee**-kohr **ayr**-kez-eek uh **voh**-nuht **paych**-ru(r)l
The train is late.	A vonat késik.	uh **voh**-nuht **kay**-sheek
Can you help me, please?	Tudna segíteni?	**tood**-nuh **she**-geet-e-nee
Can you tell me . . . ?	Meg tudna mondani . . . ?	**meg** tood-nuh **mohn**-duh-nee
I've lost my bags.	Elvesztettem a csomagjaimat.	**el**-ves-tet-tem uh **choh**-muhg-yuh-ee-muht

I've lost my money.	Elvesztettem a pénzemet.	**el**-ves-tet-tem uh **paynz**-em-et
I've lost my passport.	Elvesztettem az útlevélemet.	**el**-ves-tet-tem uhz **oot**-le-vayl-em-et
I've missed my train.	Lekéstem a vonatot.	**le**-kaysh-tem uh **voh**-nuht-oht

Menu Guide

Getting Started

waiter/waitress	pincér/pincérnő
menu	étlap
wine list	borlap
beverage list	itallap
without meat	hústalan
breakfast	reggeli
lunch	ebéd
supper	vacsora
cup/saucer	csésze/tányér
appetizers	előételek
soups	levesek
salads	saláták
vegetables	köretek
fish	halak
poultry	szárnyas
game	vadas
meat	hús
dessert	deszert
sweets	édességek
fruit	gyümölcs
beverages	italok

Breakfast

bread	kenyér
roll	zsemle
butter	vaj
jam/jelly	lekvár
warm/hot	meleg/forró
cold	hideg
milk	tej
fruit juice	gyümölcslé
eggs	tojások
hard-boiled egg	keménytojás
soft-boiled egg	lágytojás
scrambled eggs	rántotta
ham	sonka
bacon	szalonna
lemon	citrom
sugar	cukor

Appetizers, Snacks, Side Dishes

fruit salad	gyümölcs saláta
cucumber salad	uborka saláta
cheese	sajt
potatoes	burgonya
french fries	sült krumpli
rice	rízs
red cabbage	vöröskáposzta
sandwich	szendvics
Hungarian salami	téliszalami

sausage	kolbasz
frankfurter	vírsli
Hungarian biscuits	pogácsa
fried dough	lángos
cheese-filled Hungarian crepes	túróspalacsinta

Soups

bean soup	bableves
goulash soup (beef stew)	gulyásleves
cold cherry soup	meggyleves
fish stew with paprika	halászlé

Vegetables

cauliflower	karfiol
string beans	zöldbabfőzelék
potatoes	krumpli
onion	hagyma
spinach	spenót
mushroom	gomba
cabbage	káposzta
corn	kukorica
cucumber	uborka
tomato	paradicsom
stuffed cabbage	töltöttkáposzta
potato casserole	rakottkrumpli

Fish

carp	ponty
local fish	fógas
wels	harcsa

Poultry

chicken	csirke
turkey	pulyka
duck	kacsa
goose	liba
goose liver	libamáj

Meat

veal	borjú
beef	marhahús
lamb	bárány
ham	sonka
pork	sertéshús
breaded meat	rántotthús
chicken paprika	paprikáscsirke
steak	rostélyos

Desserts, Fruit

sweets	édesség
ice cream	fagylalt
whipped cream	tejszínhab
cake	torta
Hungarian crepes	palacsinta

strudel	rétes
chestnut cream	gesztenyecrém
chocolate	csokoládé
walnuts	dió
apple	alma
orange	narancs
pear	körte
sour cherries	meggy
apricot	barack
melon	dinye
layer cake with hardened, caramelized top	dobostorta

Beverages

bottle	üveg
glass	pohár
cup	csésze
beer	sör
wine	bor
white wine	fehér bor
red wine	vörös bor
brandy	pálinka
apricot brandy	barackpálinka
vodka	vodka
lemonade	limonadé
water	víz
mineral water	ásványvíz
soft drink	üditő
ice cubes	jég kockák
coffee	kávé
tea	téa
caffeine free	koffein-mentes

Index

Personal Itinerary

Departure *Date*

Time

Transportation

Arrival *Date*　*Time*

Departure *Date*　*Time*

Transportation

Accommodations

Arrival *Date*　*Time*

Departure *Date*　*Time*

Transportation

Accommodations

Arrival *Date*　*Time*

Departure *Date*　*Time*

Transportation

Accommodations

Personal Itinerary

Arrival *Date*   *Time*

Departure *Date*   *Time*

Transportation

Accommodations

Arrival *Date*   *Time*

Departure *Date*   *Time*

Transportation

Accommodations

Arrival *Date*   *Time*

Departure *Date*   *Time*

Transportation

Accommodations

Arrival *Date*   *Time*

Departure *Date*   *Time*

Transportation

Accommodations

Personal Itinerary

Arrival *Date* *Time*

Departure *Date* *Time*

Transportation

Accommodations

Arrival *Date* *Time*

Departure *Date* *Time*

Transportation

Accommodations

Arrival *Date* *Time*

Departure *Date* *Time*

Transportation

Accommodations

Arrival *Date* *Time*

Departure *Date* *Time*

Transportation

Accommodations

Addresses

Name

Address

Telephone

Name

Address

Telephone

Name

Address

Telephone

Name

Address

Telephone

Name

Address

Telephone

Name

Address

Telephone

Name

Address

Telephone

Name

Address

Telephone

Name

Address

Telephone

Name

Address

Telephone

Name

Address

Telephone

Name

Address

Telephone

Name

Address

Telephone

Name

Address

Telephone

Name

Address

Telephone

Name

Address

Telephone

Addresses

Name	*Name*
Address	*Address*
Telephone	*Telephone*
Name	*Name*
Address	*Address*
Telephone	*Telephone*
Name	*Name*
Address	*Address*
Telephone	*Telephone*
Name	*Name*
Address	*Address*
Telephone	*Telephone*
Name	*Name*
Address	*Address*
Telephone	*Telephone*
Name	*Name*
Address	*Address*
Telephone	*Telephone*
Name	*Name*
Address	*Address*
Telephone	*Telephone*
Name	*Name*
Address	*Address*
Telephone	*Telephone*

Addresses

Name	*Name*
Address	*Address*
Telephone	*Telephone*
Name	*Name*
Address	*Address*
Telephone	*Telephone*
Name	*Name*
Address	*Address*
Telephone	*Telephone*
Name	*Name*
Address	*Address*
Telephone	*Telephone*
Name	*Name*
Address	*Address*
Telephone	*Telephone*
Name	*Name*
Address	*Address*
Telephone	*Telephone*
Name	*Name*
Address	*Address*
Telephone	*Telephone*
Name	*Name*
Address	*Address*
Telephone	*Telephone*

Fodor's Travel Guides

U.S. Guides

Alaska
Arizona
Boston
California
Cape Cod, Martha's
 Vineyard, Nantucket
The Carolinas & the
 Georgia Coast
The Chesapeake
 Region
Chicago
Colorado
Disney World & the
 Orlando Area
Florida
Hawaii

Las Vegas, Reno,
 Tahoe
Los Angeles
Maine, Vermont,
 New Hampshire
Maui
Miami & the
 Keys
National Parks
 of the West
New England
New Mexico
New Orleans
New York City
New York City
 (Pocket Guide)

Pacific North Coast
Philadelphia & the
 Pennsylvania
 Dutch Country
Puerto Rico
 (Pocket Guide)
The Rockies
San Diego
San Francisco
San Francisco
 (Pocket Guide)
The South
Santa Fe, Taos,
 Albuquerque
Seattle &
 Vancouver

Texas
USA
The U. S. & British
 Virgin Islands
The Upper Great
 Lakes Region
Vacations in
 New York State
Vacations on the
 Jersey Shore
Virginia & Maryland
Waikiki
Washington, D.C.
Washington, D.C.
 (Pocket Guide)

Foreign Guides

Acapulco
Amsterdam
Australia
Austria
The Bahamas
The Bahamas
 (Pocket Guide)
Baja & Mexico's Pacific
 Coast Resorts
Barbados
Barcelona, Madrid,
 Seville
Belgium &
 Luxembourg
Berlin
Bermuda
Brazil
Budapest
Budget Europe
Canada
Canada's Atlantic
 Provinces

Cancun, Cozumel,
 Yucatan Peninsula
Caribbean
Central America
China
Czechoslovakia
Eastern Europe
Egypt
Europe
Europe's Great Cities
France
Germany
Great Britain
Greece
The Himalayan
 Countries
Holland
Hong Kong
India
Ireland
Israel
Italy

Italy 's Great Cities
Jamaica
Japan
Kenya, Tanzania,
 Seychelles
Korea
London
London
 (Pocket Guide)
London Companion
Mexico
Mexico City
Montreal &
 Quebec City
Morocco
New Zealand
Norway
Nova Scotia,
 New Brunswick,
 Prince Edward
 Island
Paris

Paris (Pocket Guide)
Portugal
Rome
Scandinavia
Scandinavian Cities
Scotland
Singapore
South America
South Pacific
Southeast Asia
Soviet Union
Spain
Sweden
Switzerland
Sydney
Thailand
Tokyo
Toronto
Turkey
Vienna & the Danube
 Valley
Yugoslavia

Wall Street Journal Guides to Business Travel

Europe

International Cities

Pacific Rim

USA & Canada

Special-Interest Guides

Bed & Breakfast and
 Country Inn Guides:
 Mid-Atlantic Region
New England
The South
The West

Cruises and Ports
 of Call
Healthy Escapes
Fodor's Flashmaps
 New York

Fodor's Flashmaps
 Washington, D.C.
Shopping in Europe
Skiing in the USA &
 Canada

Smart Shopper's
 Guide to London
Sunday in New York
Touring Europe
Touring USA